D0944639

# RUSSIAN PROSE COMPOSITION

# RUSSIAN PROSE COMPOSITION

*Annotated Passages for Translation into Russian*

BY

F. M. BORRAS
*University of Leeds*

AND

R. F. CHRISTIAN
*University of Birmingham*

OXFORD
AT THE CLARENDON PRESS
1964

*Oxford University Press, Amen House, London E.C.4*

GLASGOW NEW YORK TORONTO MELBOURNE WELLINGTON
BOMBAY CALCUTTA MADRAS KARACHI LAHORE DACCA
CAPE TOWN SALISBURY NAIROBI IBADAN ACCRA
KUALA LUMPUR HONG KONG



PRINTED IN GREAT BRITAIN

# PREFACE

THIS collection of prose extracts for translation into Russian is intended for university students and others of a comparable standard. In addition to passages from twentieth-century English authors, graded according to difficulty, it includes a number of literal translations from contemporary Russian writers for retranslation into Russian. The passages in content fall generally into the following divisions—narrative, dialogue, character, philosophical, and reflective. Every effort has been made to ensure that the English, although worthy of a university course, is reasonably straightforward and suitable for translation. Each passage is fairly fully annotated with cross-references to the authors' *Russian Syntax*, and it is hoped that the two books will serve as companion volumes for more advanced students of the Russian language.

F. M. B.
R. F. C.

# ACKNOWLEDGEMENTS

THE editors wish to thank the following for their permission to reproduce passages: Messrs. Chapman and Hall (25, *Excursion in Reality*), the owner of the copyright (29, *The Ghost*), Laurence Pollinger Ltd. and the estate of Mrs. Lawrence (32, *Sons and Lovers* and 74, *Two Blue Birds*; 33, 34, 50, 55, *The Quiet American*), Macgibbon and Kee Ltd. (35, *Portraits*), The Society of Authors representing the estate of the late Katherine Mansfield (37), Hodder and Stoughton Ltd. (38, *The Hundred Years*), Hutchinson and Co. Ltd. (39, *The Haunting of Toby Jug*), Mr. Upton Sinclair (40, 52, *Flivver King*), Rider Haggard's Executors and Macdonald and Co. (42, 43, *Montezuma's Daughter*, chapters 11 and 19), A. P. Watt and Son, Miss R. Jerome and Trinity College, Cambridge (44, 45, 56, 57, *Three Men in a Boat*; 88, *The Golden Bough*), George G. Harrap (54, *The Verdict of You All*), Martin Secker and Warburg Ltd. (60, 67, *Animal Farm*), John Murray (61, *Those without Shadows*), William Heinemann Ltd. (65, 66, *The Forsyte Saga*; 71, *The Devil's Cub*; 26, 30, 53, 86, *The Summing Up*, *The Razor's Edge*, *The Moon and Sixpence*), Chatto and Windus Ltd. (75, *The Living Novel*; 87, *Civilization*; 99, *Point Counter Point*), Miss D. E. Collins, Cassell and Co. Ltd. (78, *The Gathering Storm*), Routledge and Kegan Paul Ltd. (82, *History of Russian Literature*; 100, *A Coat of Many Colours*), Hamish Hamilton Ltd. (72, 73, *Mistress to an Age*), Eyre and Spottiswoode Ltd. (76, *Napoleon*), Victor Gollancz Ltd. (85, *The Case of the Gilded Fly*), Macmillan and Co. Ltd. (51, *The Two Solitudes*; 89, *The Masters*), The Society of Authors (94, *Left Hand, Right Hand*), The Observer (93), and The Guardian (77, 92).

We would like to express our thanks to the following colleagues and friends who have given their opinions from time to time on points of modern Russian usage: Mrs. A. Arian, Dr. I. Baykov, Mr. L. Ross, Mrs. V. S. Coe, Mrs. L. Shorrocks, Mrs. Z. P. Garkunova, and Miss T. Cizova.

*R.S.* numbers refer to paragraph references in *Russian Syntax*, by F. M. Borras and R. F. Christian (Oxford, Clarendon Press, 1959)

# 1

After leaving[1] school recently I started looking for a job[2] where my knowledge of Russian would be useful. After looking[1] through the advertisements in the papers I went to an office in the middle of town. I had to[3] wait quite a long time but eventually I was taken to the secretary's room, and he asked[4] me to fill up a form. Then he started asking[4] me whether I spoke[5] Russian well, whether I knew any other languages, and so on. In the end he offered me a job as a typist,[6] saying that he was sure I would get promotion in the near future since I was very well qualified, and all that was required was to get[7] some experience.

The conditions are good—not too many hours and good pay[8]—so I gladly accepted and started work on the first of May. There are twelve of us in the department:[9] the head of the department, his assistant, a secretary, an accountant, a bookkeeper, and several other employees. I'm mainly concerned with translations from Russian to English and vice versa, especially technical translations. It was rather difficult at first and I had to[3] use[10] the dictionary a lot, but I have got used to it now and it is much easier.

The subject of this passage is a woman.

1 Past gerund.

2 иска́ть+acc.; she intends to get a definite job, although she does not know exactly what it will be. *R.S.* 32 (*b*).

3 Note the frequency of the verb приходи́ться (прийти́сь) in this meaning.

4 *R.S.* 332.

5 говорю́ ли я. Here and elsewhere in this passage care is needed with the tenses. *R.S.* 209.

[6] ме́сто машини́стки.

[7] Say 'and all I lacked was practical experience'. *R.S.* 302.

[8] 'Pay', meaning 'wages', is often translated by зарпла́та, which is a contraction of за́работная пла́та. It should not be confused with запла́та 'a patch'.

[9] Say 'in our department there are twelve people'.

[10] по́льзоваться (воспо́льзоваться)+instr. means primarily 'to take advantage of', 'to derive benefit from', and will be appropriate here. Note the cognate verb испо́льзовать, which is both imperfective and perfective, and governs the accusative case. прибега́ть к may be used as an alternative to по́льзоваться.

## 2

Opposite our house lived a wealthy old merchant, who was reputed to be[1] a very clever man and the owner of a large collection of books. Somehow or other he had learned[2] from my parents that I was[3] a diligent boy and was very fond of reading, but since my parents were too poor to buy me books, I had nothing to read.[4] One day he sent someone round to fetch me.[5] After inquiring what I read, whether I understood it all, and what I remembered, the old man seemed very pleased and made me a present of Tolstoy's *Childhood, Boyhood, and Youth.* What happiness! I was so glad that I cried for joy,[6] and after thanking the old man warmly, I ran off[7] home as fast as I could. Fearing that[8] someone might take[9] my present from me I ran straight upstairs to the nursery, took off[9] my shoes, lay on my bed, started reading, and promptly forgot about everything else. Some time later my mother found me still lying[10] there with the book in my hand. She thought I had gone mad. I did not say a word, did not understand what was said to me, and would not go down to supper.

[1] Among the various possibilities are слыл + instr. (or за+acc.); име́л репута́цию + gen.; and по́льзовался репута́цией.

[2] i.e. 'had got to know'.

[3] See Passage 1, note 4.

[4] *R.S.* 522.

[5] за+instr.

[6] *R.S.* 622. [7] *R.S.* 232. [8] *R.S.* 265.

[9] Compare the verbs отнима́ть (отня́ть) and снима́ть (снять). The former corresponds to 'take away' in the sense of 'deprive', the latter to 'take off' in the sense of 'remove' (e.g. a hat, a coat, shoes).

[10] Instr. predicate: заста́ла меня́ всё ещё лежа́щим.

## 3

A[1] boy from a big town once visited his cousin who lived in the country. They were both the same age[2] and soon became good friends. The boy from town said to his new friend: 'When you come[3] to our town I'll show you buildings ten stories[4] high, new factories, and wonderful shops. I'll take you along the main streets where even at night it's as bright as in broad daylight.'[5] To this his country cousin replied: 'And I'll show you woods and take you to places where[6] you can pick berries, mushrooms, and nuts. And we can spend our days in green fields where thousands of different coloured flowers grow. And best of all, I'll find you a bird's nest[7] with eggs in it.' The boy from town then asked: 'But what will you teach me?'[8] 'I'll teach you to[8] plough the land, dig potatoes,[9] and graze cattle. And, besides, I'll teach you to climb[10] high trees without a ladder, and to cross streams without bridges.' His friend replied: 'It's very useful to learn all this: but I'll teach you something even better: I'll teach you to read books. And books will teach you everything you want to know.'

[1] The article should be translated here. *R.S.* 464.

[2] *R.S.* 518. [3] Future tense.

[4] Make a compound adjective from де́сять and эта́ж. *R.S.* 750 (vi).

[5] *R.S.* 135. [6] туда́, где. *R.S.* 392. [7] *R.S.* 149 (i).

[8] To teach someone *to do* something may be translated by one of the three verbs учи́ть (научи́ть), обуча́ть (обучи́ть), and вы́учивать (вы́учить), followed by the acc. of the person and the infinitive. The thing taught, if expressed by a noun, will go in the dative case: *R.S.* 43. Compare the verbs приуча́ть (приучи́ть), which means 'to train', 'school', or 'discipline' someone to do something, and проу́чивать

(проучи́ть), which means 'to teach' in the sense of 'to give a severe lesson to', 'to punish': e.g. 'I'll teach you!' я проучу́ вас!

[9] Use the singular. *R.S.* 15 (i).

[10] влеза́ть (влезть) на+acc.

# 4

It was night; and in a little country-house a gentleman went to bed. His servant, Rama, was sleeping on the floor near his bed.

'Rama, Rama,' cried the master. 'Is it raining? Go and[1] see.'

The master repeated[2] his question many times because it was very difficult to wake up Rama. Then Rama rubbed[3] his eyes, clapped his hands,[4] and answered: 'It is raining, master.'

'How do you know?' asked the master.

'The cat came in,' answered Rama.

'But how does that prove that it is raining?'

'I felt its coat,[5] sir,' said Rama, 'and it was wet.'

'All right!' said the master. 'Will you put out the lamp? I cannot sleep with the light.'[6]

'Well, sir,' said Rama, 'you cover your face with the sheet and it will be dark.'

'You are a lazy fellow,' said the master. 'Go, shut the door.'

'Master,' said Rama, 'I did two things for you.[7] Now it is your turn.'

As soon as Rama said this, he turned over and fell asleep.

[1] Omit.

[2] *R.S.* 197 (ii).

[3] In this sense of rubbing the eyes on awakening, протира́ть (протере́ть). This verb also means 'to wear through' (by rubbing), and its reflexive form means 'to be worn through': рукава́ протёрлись на локтя́х 'the sleeves are worn through at the elbows'.

[4] хло́пнул в ладо́ши. Notice the prepositional construction in

Russian, where English uses a direct object. The word ладо́ши exists only in this expression. It is the plural diminutive form of ладо́нь ('palm of the hand').

[5] шерсть, meaning 'the hair or fur of an animal', is the correct word here; cf. шерсть соба́ки, шерсть овцы́. Шку́ра means 'the hide of a dead animal'; cf. волк в ове́чьей шку́ре 'a wolf in sheep's clothing'. Мех, 'fur', means the processed hide.

[6] при све́те. [7] Say 'I have rendered you two services'.

## 5

I was driving the car[1] myself, as my wife, who usually drives, was not feeling well.[2] It was getting dark and my fingers were aching from the cold. I was in a great hurry. All of a sudden a policeman stopped me. 'Surely[3] you know you're not allowed to do more than thirty miles an hour[4] here?' he said. 'It's dangerous to travel fast along this road. There's a school not far from here and children are often crossing the road. An accident can easily happen.'

I said I was sorry and that I didn't know I was driving[5] so fast.

'Well, be more careful another time,'[6] he said, 'otherwise[7] you'll find yourself[8] in trouble.'

I thanked him and, after a moment's pause, added:

'Since you stopped me, can I ask you how to get to[8] Birmingham?'

'Keep straight on[9] along this road for another twenty-five miles. Then you'll cross a stone bridge and see a cross-roads. On the right of the cross-roads is a big garage. Turn[10] left there and you'll be in Birmingham in an hour's time.'[11]

I followed his instructions but there was so much traffic that I was an hour and a half late for my appointment.[12]

[1] For the construction with the verbs пра́вить or управля́ть see *R.S.* 47 (i); води́ть (вести́) маши́ну is an alternative expression for 'to drive a car'. [2] *R.S.* 258.

[3] i.e. 'can it be that you do not know?' ра́зве вы не зна́ете?

[4] Quite literally де́лать бо́льше тридцати́ миль в час.

[5] Here simply use е́хать, as no complement is expressed.

[6] в друго́й раз.

[7] *R.S.* 405.

[8] In both these contexts the idiomatic verb попада́ть (попа́сть) в+acc. may be used.

[9] поезжа́йте пря́мо.

[10] *R.S.* 354. One can say either поверни́те or сверни́те.

[11] *R.S.* 538.

[12] я на полтора́ часа́ опозда́л на свида́ние. Note that на with the expression of time cannot be omitted even though it recurs in the same clause.

# 6

The Wind said to the Sun one day, 'You are more beautiful than I am, but I am stronger than you.'

'Oh, no!' said the Sun. 'You are not stronger than I.'

They looked down and saw a man. He was walking quickly along[1] the road. 'Do you see that man on the road?' said the Wind. 'He has a coat on.[2] Can you take it off him? I know I can do so, but I am sure you cannot. You are not strong enough.'[3]

'I think I can,' said the Sun.

'Well,' said the Wind, 'if you can do so and I can't, you[4] are stronger than I am. If I can do so and you can't, then I am stronger than you. Am I right?'

'Yes,' answered the Sun. 'You are right. If you make the man take his coat off, you are stronger than I am. If I make him take it off, I am stronger than you. You try first.'

'All right,' said the Wind. 'I'll show you.'

So the Wind began to blow.[5] The air became colder and colder. The man held his coat with both hands.

'I am glad I have my coat on,' he thought.

The Wind blew and blew,[6] but he could not blow the man's coat off.[7] At last he was tired[8] and said to the Sun, 'It's your turn now, I am tired.'

It was evening already, but the Sun began to shine. The air became warmer and warmer.

The man smiled. 'There is no wind now,' he thought, 'and I am very warm. I must take my coat off, or[9] I shall be too hot.'

Then the man took his coat off.

[1] *R.S.* 586. [2] Say 'on him is a coat'. [3] *R.S.* 427.
[4] Say 'then you are . . .'. [5] *R.S.* 233. [6] Quite literally.
[7] сдуть, cf. further down, 'take off' снять.
[8] The verb уставáть (устáть) means 'to grow tired'. Thus он устáл can mean 'he is tired' or 'he was tired' (i.e. 'he has (had) become tired'), according to the context. The adjective устáлый ('tired') can only be used attributively: устáлая жéнщина 'a tired woman'.
[9] *R.S.* 405.

# 7

This is the story[1] the children told. They were sitting by the river, watching the candle. Soon it went out. They were so unhappy that they were not able to talk any more. Then they fell asleep. When they woke, they were hungry and weak.

Once they heard a cry far away. Tom shouted back[2] but no one replied. They listened[3] again but they heard nothing more. They went slowly back to the little river. Then they slept again. When they woke they were terribly hungry.

'What day is it, Tom?' asked Becky.

'I think it is Wednesday,' said Tom, 'or maybe Thursday. I don't know.'

At last Tom said: 'Becky, I am going to look for a way out.'

'Oh, Tom, don't leave me,'[4] said Becky. 'I don't want to die alone.'

'Becky, I must. I have a string in my pocket. I shall tie[5] one end of the string to this rock and hold[6] the other end in my hand. Then I shall be able to come back to you.'

So he left Becky and started. He went along[7] one corridor and then another to the end of the string.[8] He was going to turn back when[9] far away he saw a small blue spot. It looked like daylight. He threw down the string and moved towards the spot. Then he pushed his head and shoulders through a small hole and saw the great river.

MARK TWAIN (*adapted*)

[1] Вот что рассказа́ли. [2] отозва́лся.

[3] Use прислу́шиваться (прислу́шаться), which means 'to listen attentively in order to hear'.

[4] Say 'don't go away from me'. *R.S.* 214.

[5] The verb завя́зывать (завяза́ть) is used, meaning 'to tie a knot' (у́зел). Here the meaning of 'tie to' can be expressed by the prefix при-, cf. привяза́ть соба́ку к забо́ру 'to tie the dog to the fence'. The verb свя́зывать (связа́ть) means 'to tie together'; cf. the figurative связа́ть концы́ с конца́ми 'to make ends meet'.

[6] The sense here is continuous. Aspect?

[7] Perfective aspect.

[8] Say 'until the string was finished' or 'until he had unwound all the string'. [9] *R.S.* 383 (ii).

## 8

Tom went back to Becky and told her that he had found a way out. At first she did not believe him and did not want to go with him!

'I am going to die,[1] and I want to die,' she said.

But at last she moved a little.[2] Tom helped her. She was very weak and could not walk.[3] But when she saw the blue spot of daylight, she became stronger[4] at once. They got out of the hole one after the other. They sat on the grass and looked at the river and the sunshine and the forest. They were so happy that they cried and cried.

Then they saw some men in a boat. Tom shouted to them and they stopped. At first the men did not believe the children's story. The hole was very far from the[5] place where the cave was.

But at last they had to[6] believe the story. The children's faces were so thin, and they were so weak. The men took them to a house[7] and gave them supper.[8] After that they told the children to lie down and rest.

They fell asleep at once and nobody wanted to wake them. At last, when it was night, the men took them home in their boat.

MARK TWAIN (*adapted*)

[1] Say 'I shall die . . .'.
[2] Say 'made a small movement'. [3] *R.S.* 286.
[4] к ней вернýлись сúлы. The verb крéпнуть (окрéпнуть) means to regain strength after an illness. [5] *R.S.* 468.
[6] See Passage 1, note 9. [7] *R.S.* 464.
[8] Use an infinitive after дáли. *R.S.* 231.

## 9

'Take him into this room,' said the woman, and opened the door into a small bedroom.

Eliza put the child on the bed, and he fell asleep at once. Then she went to the window and looked at the river. Great pieces of ice[1] were moving slowly down it.

'How can I get to[2] the other side?' she said[3] again and again. 'I must get over the river tonight with my child.'

Suddenly she heard a shout. She looked up and saw Sam. Haley and Andy were a little behind him[4] and could not see her.

'Oh, they've found me,' she cried.

It was a terrible moment for poor Eliza. There was no time to think.[5] The room had a door[6] which opened towards the river. So she picked up the child, left the room through this door and ran to[7] the river. Haley saw her. He jumped off his horse, shouted to Sam and Andy and ran after[7] her. The next moment[8] Eliza was on the bank of the river.

Haley and the two slaves came fast behind her. Then with a terrible cry she jumped onto a great piece of ice. But she did not stay on it for a moment. She jumped to another piece, and then another. She fell, but got up on her feet again.

She lost her shoes, and the ice cut her feet. But at last she came to the other side. There a man helped her to get up the bank out of the water.[9]

Haley was very angry but Sam and Andy were glad that Eliza had got away. They laughed and shouted with[10] joy. Then they jumped onto their horses and went home as fast as they could.

HARRIET BEECHER STOWE (*adapted*)

1 'Piece of ice' льди́на.
2 Use an infinitive construction.
3 Say 'repeated'.
4 бежа́ли вслед за ним.
5 *R.S.* 301 and 521.
6 Say 'The door of the room opened towards' (выходи́ла на).
7 Use perfective verbs 'set off running'. *R.S.* 232.
8 в оди́н миг.
9 Say 'to get out of the water onto the bank'.
10 *R.S.* 622.

## 10

When visiting a certain town on business recently, I quite unexpectedly bumped into[1] an old friend of mine[2] in the street. He had always been a great art lover and was justifiably[3] proud of[4] two marvellous pictures by a sixteenth-century Spanish master which he owned—one a woman's head, the other an old man with a long black beard. He had recently bought three expensive and very rare Eastern carpets, he informed me. His flat seemed to contain everything—rare books and paintings, gold coins, silver cups and plates—not to mention[5] a magnificent bronze statue which stands in the hall. I lunched with him and then he took me to look round[6] an early eighteenth-century[7] house nearby.[8] It reminded me very much of a small palace in Leningrad, in the shadow of which I spent my childhood. What a magnificent city it is with its palaces, cathedrals, and bridges over rivers and canals. Shall I ever again see[9] the statue of Peter the Great astride his horse on the banks of the Neva, or saunter[10] by the river on the white nights in spring, or gaze in awe at the great fortress where so many innocent men perished?

[1] In this familiar sense ста́лкиваться (столкну́ться) с + instr. may be used.
[2] See Passage 3, note 1.
[3] справедли́во or по пра́ву.
[4] *R.S.* 48.
[5] не говоря́ уже́ о.
[6] The appropriate verbal prefix is о-. Use an imperfective verb because the course, not the result, of the action is meant.
[7] *R.S.* 30.
[8] находя́щийся побли́зости (place before the noun).
[9] Work in the impersonal verb приводи́ться (привести́сь).
[10] прогу́ливаться (прогуля́ться) when the meaning, as here, is 'to walk up and down in a leisurely manner'.

## 11

During that spring and summer, she thought Speke had[1] a beauty and sweetness of its own, although it was very different[2] from the kind of country[3] she loved most. She looked on meadows scarlet with flowers.[4] Every morning she heard the singing of a great choir of birds. And the song of the nightingale could be heard[5] even in the dawn.

Mary's energy was not satisfied with such work[6] as she did in the house and garden, and she began to do a good deal of work in the village. In July she succeeded in organizing a little school. By the end of the year[7] she had nine scholars, to whom she taught reading and writing, and who learned prayers[8] under her direction. She wrote to Jane that she had one very bright scholar, some very tolerable, and two or three very bad. Those who lived near came to her every[9] Wednesday and Saturday evening. On Sunday her hours were from nine till eleven, then from one to three, and from four to half-past five. These were small beginnings,[10] but Mary was always hoping to have a larger school with a class for the villagers.

[1] Use имéть. *R.S.* 339.

[2] отличáться can be qualified by óчень or by во мнóгом, but not by мнóго by itself.

[3] прирóда would be appropriate in this sense of 'the land and all its natural phenomena'.

[4] It is best to say 'on which showed scarlet (алéли) the flowers'.

[5] *R.S.* 303.

[6] Say 'her work in . . . did not exhaust all her energy'.

[7] *R.S.* 549.

[8] учи́ли моли́твы. Cf. the use of учи́ть in the meaning of 'teach' in Passage 3, note 8.

[9] *R.S.* 542.

[10] Use the singular: это бы́ло тóлько скрóмное начáло.

## 12

Thank goodness they were not far from home.[1] It seemed to John that his nose was[2] freezing and that he could not feel his fingers any more. It was so dark that he was afraid he might[3] lose his way. The two friends walked on in silence until[4] they came to a telephone box. John stopped and, turning to his friend, said: 'I promised Tom I would[5] ring up his wife and tell her not to wait dinner for him.[6] I don't know his number, but I'll look it up[7] in the telephone book. I shan't be a minute.'[8] After passing on the message, John joined his friend again. They wondered if they should stop the night[9] at an hotel in the next street, since the weather was so terrible. They were a long time deciding[10] but in the end they made up their minds to try and reach home. As they walked past the gates of a factory it struck[11] nine. Just as they were thinking that they would not be home before midnight, a bus drew up on the opposite side of the road. Despite the snow the driver had evidently managed to keep going and John and his friend got on board.[12]

[1] им недалеко́ до́ дому. [2] See Passage 1, note 4.
[3] Use the infinitive. [4] *R.S.* 390 (i).
[5] Use the infinitive. [6] ждать его́ к обе́ду.
[7] Say, 'I'll have a look in . . . .' Remember that such English expressions can often be translated by a single Russian perfective verb.
[8] Say 'It will take only a minute'.
[9] Follow the verb разду́мывать by a dative and negative intive construction, incorporating ли (e.g. не переночева́ть or не finiановиться ли им . . .). [10] *R.S.* 228. [11] *R.S.* 769.
ост се́ли в авто́бус.

## 13

Air, warmth, food, clothing, and housing are necessary to a man for his existence, and are sometimes called his first requisites.[1] However, we can all live even if[2] we do not drink wine, eat cakes, or wear silk clothes. And so these things are not first requisites for a man; they are not indispensable for his existence and only show his wealth. A man who is very tired sleeps peacefully even on the bare floor: but probably it is more pleasant for him to sleep on a soft bed. On a hard[3] stool one can sit and rest very well: but without doubt it is more comfortable and pleasant to sit on a soft chair. A coat of the coarsest cloth does us great service,[4] for it protects us from the cold, the wind, and the rain, but indisputably it is more pleasant to have a coat of fine cloth, with beautiful buttons. Therefore soft beds, easy chairs, and expensive dress do not belong to[5] the first requisites, but to the pleasures and comforts of life. If we have wholesome food in sufficient quantity, decent clothing, and a good dwelling-house, let us be[6] satisfied. Such should be the philosophy of all wise men.

[1] предме́ты пе́рвой необходи́мости. [2] Say 'if even'.
[3] жёсткий. *R.S.* 167.
[4] Say 'has many useful functions' (примене́ния).
[5] Say 'cannot be considered'.
[6] For 1st person plural imperatives in general see *R.S.* 216.

## 14

I well remember my first meeting with Olga. Even now after all these years her portrait, which you see hanging[1] over there on the wall, always reminds me of that cold autumn morning in 1894. It had rained the previous evening, and damp leaves lay on the path which led through the dense forest to the Count's estate. The rays of the sun barely penetrated the network of branches. A few sparrows flew overhead, and somewhere nearby the sound of[2] a brook could be heard.[3] I was walking along when suddenly[4] I stopped. In front of me through the light mist I could see[3] a white figure. For a second an absurd thought that it might be a ghost entered my head, and I couldn't help trembling. Something in the atmosphere of the place was getting on my nerves.[5] I went on slowly along the muddy path and approached the figure. It was a woman[6] of about twenty-five. She was smiling at me—a strange, tender smile.[7] She was dressed in a light blue skirt and white blouse, and was wearing a hat made of silk material with a large feather on the top. She put out her hand and said: 'You must be the new schoolmaster.' She looked me straight in the eyes, was silent for a few seconds,[8] and then added: 'You remind me in some strange way of my nephew. You have the same walk[9] and the same face.' She laughed. 'Even your moustache is like his: it needs trimming.'[10]

1 Say 'which, as you see, is hanging'.
2 *R.S.* 97.
3 *R.S.* 303.
4 я шёл . . . и вдруг . . .
5 де́йствовало мне на не́рвы.
6 *R.S.* 23.
7 Instrumental case.
8 Use по- prefix. *R.S.* 231.
9 *R.S.* 116.
10 Use the verb подстрига́ть (подстри́чь) and remember that 'moustache' is plural in Russian.

# 15

I had bought a ticket at Milan for[1] Stresa. I had also bought a new hat. As I sat in the compartment and looked out of the window, the new hat felt very new and the clothes very old. I myself felt as sad[2] as the wet Lombard country[3] that was outside through the window.[4] I had the paper but I did not read it because I did not want to read about the war. I was going to forget about the war. I felt very lonely and I was glad when the train got to Stresa. At the station I had expected to see the porters from the hotels, but there was no one. The season had been over a long time and no one met the train. I got down from the train with my bag, it was very light to carry,[5] being empty except for[6] two shirts, and stood in the rain[7] while the train went on.[8] I found a man in the station and asked him if he knew[9] what hotels were open. The Grand Hotel was open and several small hotels that stayed open all the year.[10] I started[11] in the rain, carrying my bag. I saw a carriage coming down the street and signalled to the driver. It is better to arrive in a carriage. We drove up to the entrance of the big hotel and the concierge came out with an umbrella and was very polite. I took a good room: it was very big and light and looked out on the lake.

[1] биле́т в. [2] уны́лый can refer to both people and things.

[3] ме́стность ('the area round about', 'locality', 'terrain'), or possibly приро́да: see Passage 11, note 3.

[4] за окно́м ваго́на: i.e. 'on the other side of the window'.

[5] Quite literally: его́ бы́ло о́чень легко́ нести́.

[6] Either say 'empty with the exception of' за исключе́нием + gen., or 'there was nothing in it except' в нём ничего́ не́ было кро́ме + gen.; but not пусто́й кро́ме. [7] под дождём.

[8] пока́ по́езд отходи́л is one possibility (i.e. 'he stood there as it was going out').

[9] See Passage 1, note 4.

[10] кру́глый год. NB. я проспа́л кру́глые су́тки 'I slept the clock round'. [11] я пусти́лся в путь.

## 16

Dear Mother,

I'm sorry I haven't written for so long. If you didn't know before you must realize now that being a student[1] in the faculty of medicine[2] is no easy matter. I get up very early now, and go to bed about eleven. Five hours a day are spent on lectures and classes alone.[3] There are labs., clinics, and reading besides. The professors tell us that we must show initiative, that it isn't enough for a student to attend lectures regularly[4] and take notes on[5] what he hears there. We are given long booklists which we have to read, understand, and remember.[6] During the week I have no time[7] to go to the theatre or the pictures. I can't even allow myself the luxury of paying visits[8] every Saturday or Sunday.

I have a very nice, clean, light room. It's so big that I work there as well as[9] sleep. With the £10[10] uncle gave me I bought a big solid writing desk. I get a bed, cupboard, and three chairs from the landlady and that's all I need. The landlady says that if you would like to come and see how I'm getting on,[11] she'll put[12] an extra[13] bed in my room. There's plenty of room. Why not come[14] for a few days? I'd be so glad to see you.

With love from

Mary

1 Use the infinitive: быть студе́нткой.
2 на not в with факульте́т. *R.S.* 560.
3 ухо́дят на одни́ . . .
4 аккура́тно.
5 запи́сывать, что . . .
6 Use the perfective infinitives of the three verbs after должны́.
7 *R.S.* 522.
8 таку́ю ро́скошь как ходи́ть в го́сти.
9 не то́лько . . . но и.
10 на+acc. See somewhat similar examples in *R.S.* 655.
11 как я живу́.
12 'Put standing': поста́вит.
13 ещё.
14 Use the infinitive with бы: почему́ бы тебе́ не прие́хать; and see *R.S.* 272.

# 17

The air was frosty, the moon was bright,[1] and it was very pleasant; we came through a village, then through a dark wood, then uphill, then downhill,[2] till after an eight miles' run[3] we came to the town, through the streets and into the Market Place. It was all quite still except for[4] the clatter[5] of the horse's hoofs on the stones—everybody was asleep. The church clock[6] struck three[7] as we drew up at Doctor White's door. John rang the bell twice, and then knocked at the door like thunder.[8] A window was flung open,[9] and Doctor White, in his nightcap, put his head out and said, 'What do you want?'

'Mrs. Gordon is very ill, sir; master wants you to go at once, for he thinks she will die if you cannot get there—here is a note.'

'Wait,' he said, 'I will come.'

He shut the window, and was soon at the door.

'The worst of it is,' he said, 'that my horse has been out[10] all day and is quite done up; my son has just been sent for,[11] and he has taken the other. What is to be done? Can I have your horse?'

'He has come up at a gallop[12] nearly all the way, sir, and I was to give him a rest here; but I think my master would not be against it if you think fit, sir.'

'All right,' he said, 'I will soon be ready.'

ANNA SEWELL

[1] Use the long form of the adjective, луна́ была́ я́ркая, or, more idiomatically in Russian, say луна́ я́рко сия́ла. [2] *R.S.* 599.

[3] Say 'and finally, having travelled eight miles'. *R.S.* 243.

[4] [5] Say 'All was quiet, only the horse's hoofs clattered on' (цо́кали по). [6] часы́ на це́ркви. [7] *R.S.* 769.

[8] The comparison might possibly be expressed by a verb—e.g. забараба́нил в дверь.

[9] распа́хивать (распахну́ть) conveys the strong sense of 'flinging open': окно́ распахну́лось. [10] Say 'has carried me'.

[11] 'To send for a doctor' is вызыва́ть (вы́звать).

[12] она шла гало́пом.

## 18

I am very sorry I can't tell you this little boy's name and where he lives and who his father and mother are. I didn't even manage to make his face out[1] properly in the dark.[2] I only remember that his nose was freckled[3] and that his trousers were very short.

One summer's day I went into a little garden—I don't know the name of it—on the Vasilevsky island, near a white church. I had an interesting book with me, and I sat on and on, engrossed in my reading,[4] and didn't notice evening come on.[5] When spots began to appear before my eyes[6] and it became quite difficult to read, I shut the book with a bang,[7] got up, and started walking towards the exit. The garden was already empty and lights were winking[8] in the streets.

I was afraid the garden would be closed, and I walked very quickly. Suddenly I stopped. Behind the bushes to one side I seemed to hear[9] somebody crying. I turned into a side walk, and there in the darkness was a small white stone house[10] such as there are in all town gardens—a keeper's lodge.[11] A little boy of seven or eight was standing by the wall, hanging his head[12] and crying loudly and disconsolately. I went up and called out to him:

'Hey, what's the matter?'

'Nothing.'

'What do you mean, nothing? Has somebody hurt you?'

'No.'

'Then what are you crying for?'

It was still difficult for him to talk. He still hadn't choked down[13] all his tears. And so he remained silent.

*Translated and adapted from* L. PANTELEEV

[1] Use the perfective verb разглядéть and cf. расслы́шать 'to make out by ear'. *R.S.* 687.

[2] Begin the sentence with 'in the dark'.

[3] *R.S.* 687.

[4] This is a rather cumbersome translation of two characteristic Russian verbs in which the basic roots are combined with the prefix за- and the suffix -ся in the meaning of 'to do something for a long time (or too long a time)': i.e. я засиде́лся, зачита́лся. Cf. зарабо́таться до но́чи 'to burn the midnight oil'; задержа́ться 'to stay too long'. These perfective verbs make their own imperfectives.

[5] как наступи́л ве́чер.

[6] у меня́ зарябило в глаза́х. Cf. in a similar meaning у меня́ пестри́ло в глаза́х.

[7] Use the verb захло́пывать (захло́пнуть).

[8] A translation of мелька́ть (мелькну́ть), basically 'to flash momentarily'.

[9] мне послы́шалось. See *R.S.* 310 for idiomatic uses of the reflexive particle -ся.

[10] An attempt to render the idiomatic беле́ть 'to show white'. Russian says 'a house showed white', meaning it was white and it was also visible. These verbs in -еть, denoting colours, are often prefixed by за- in the meaning of 'to come into view'. See *R.S.* 236.

[11] сторо́жка.

[12] Past gerund (опусти́в).

[13] Use the verb прогла́тывать (проглоти́ть).

# 19

Sitting down to tea in the evening, Semyon Semyonovich listened with a vacant air[1] to his wife who was jotting something down on a bit of paper[2] and saying happily:

'It will be nice and cheap. Four bottles of wine, a litre of vodka, two tins[3] of anchovies, three hundred grammes of salmon and ham. Then I'll make a spring salad with fresh cucumbers and I'll cook a kilo of sausages.'

'Well, fancy that.'[4]

'Did you say something?'

'I said "Well, fancy that".'

'Is there something you don't like?' asked his wife anxiously.[5]

'Yes, there is,' replied Semyon Semyonovich drily. 'For example, I don't like the fact that each cucumber costs one rouble fifteen copecks.'

'But two cucumbers will do[6] for the whole salad you know.'

'Yes, yes, cucumbers, salmon, anchovies. Do you know how much it will all come to?'

'I don't understand you, Semyon. It's my name-day, there'll be guests coming, we haven't done any entertaining[7] for two years now, but we're continually going out to everybody else's[8]—it's very awkward.'

'Why awkward?'

'Awkward because it's not polite.'

'Well, all right,' Semyon Semyonovich said wearily. 'Give me the list here. There look, we cross out all this. And all that's left . . . as a matter of fact[9] there's nothing left at all, Katya, just you buy a bottle of vodka and 150 grammes of herring. Anyone[10] will tell you herring is the classic hors-d'œuvre.'

'Semyon, there'll be a scandal.'

'Very well then, in that case get another tin of sprats. Only don't get Leningrad sprats; ask for Tula ones.[11] Although they're cheaper, they're much more nutritious.'

*Translated and adapted from* I. ILF AND E. PETROV

1 со скуча́ющим ви́дом.

2 Use the diminutive бума́жка to translate 'a bit of'.

3 Literally 'boxes': коро́бочки.

4 This is an approximate translation of здра́вствуйте, which is here used as an exclamation signifying unwelcome surprise.

5 Two English words are needed to translate the Russian verb забеспоко́илась.

6 пойдёт на + acc. See *R.S.* 656 for some similar examples where на translates 'for'.

7 The Russian is ничего́ не устра́ивали: 'haven't laid anything on', 'haven't organized anything' in this special sense of a party.

8 Use the versatile verb быва́ть.

9 One of the many possible translations of the idiomatic со́бственно.

10 Say 'everyone': вся́кий (or ка́ждый). *R.S.* 497.

11 Omit 'ones'.

## 20

In her student days Lena had had many friends, but now she often felt lonely.[1] There was nobody to talk to.[2] She now longed to be with[3] people with experience of life,[4] and she used to tease herself and say—fancy me a teacher, still wanting[5] someone to teach me! Until last year one of the most remarkable men in the town used to work at her school. Everyone treated him with[6] respect: he was a hero of the First World War: he was an outstanding teacher. Lena considered him her saviour. At first she had been all at sea;[7] the children were naughty during lessons and wouldn't obey her. She used to cry at night. But Andrew had helped her. He had revealed to her what matters most:[8] that a schoolchild is just like a grown-up. No two are alike.[9] You need to understand them and to earn[10] their confidence. He talked to her as if she were his own daughter. She could not go through a day without hearing[11] a few words from him. But last winter he had been taken seriously ill.[12] The doctors said it was heart trouble and had stopped him working.[13] True he was feeling better now and he would sometimes drop in at school but Lena could not bring herself to[14] bother him with her own problems. It was time to stand on her own feet, she thought. After all, she was getting on for thirty,[15] she wasn't a girl any more. Still it was difficult when there was nobody to consult.[2]

*Adapted from* I. EHRENBURG

[1] тоскова́ла. [2] не́ с кем + infinitive. *R.S.* 522.
[3] её тяну́ло к . . . 'she was drawn towards', 'attracted to'. Cf. меня́ тя́нет домо́й 'I'm longing to go home'.
[4] Use an adjective.
[5] Say 'a teacher . . . but still I want . . .'.
[6] относи́лись к . . . с . . . [7] совсе́м растеря́лась.
[8] са́мое гла́вное. [9] Say 'one is not like another'.
[10] *R.S.* 34. [11] Say 'live through . . . not having heard'.

[12] *R.S.* 234. Use тяжело́ with the verb.

[13] Use запреща́ть (запрети́ть) with the infinitive. For other uses of 'to stop' see *R.S.* 352.

[14] не реша́лась.

[15] ей ведь ско́ро три́дцать.

# 21

'Dear Mary,

Congratulations! If you come to Moscow, I shall try and see you. I can't imagine at all[1] what you are like[2] these days. I must confess, though, I don't understand your letter. You speak too lightly about matters of importance. It's understandable that you should want to see Moscow again. You and your husband will be interested to see another world.[3] But don't think that just because you were born in Moscow you will feel at home here. It's not your fault that your mother took you away to Belgium as a girl, but do be serious and try and understand that you'll only feel a tourist,[4] a foreigner, in your native town. Even if you were here and could see with your own eyes what we have accomplished, you still[5] wouldn't understand a thing. It's a completely different world. Why did it all begin here and not, say, in Belgium? Probably we had less bread and more courage . . .'

He put down his pen and stared gloomily at the sheet of paper. His hands were trembling. Does she need my explanations, he thought. Let her live her own life,[6] and do as she pleases. I'll send a telegram, congratulate her, and that's all. And he tore[7] his unfinished letter[8] into pieces, threw it in the fire and sadly shook his head.[9]

*Adapted from* I. EHRENBURG

[1] ника́к не могу́.

[2] кака́я ты.

[3] *R.S.* 130.

[4] ты бу́дешь чу́вствовать себя́ + instr. Use the feminine form of the noun.

[5] ты всё равно́.

[6] For 3rd person singular imperatives see *R.S.* 219. For the case of the noun see *R.S.* 52 (iii).

[7] изорва́л на клочки́. Either на or в may be used. The imper-

fective form изрыва́ть is not used in this meaning.

[8] недопи́санное письмо́. [9] *R.S.* 51.

# 22

He was mistaken in thinking that Saburov's fortunes had undergone no changes.[1] True the Saburovs lived in the same cramped little room, even more cluttered up with[2] pictures than ever, and Glasha's modest wage still remained the basis of their budget.[3] But the Saburovs' life had changed a great deal.[4]

It had all begun with[5] Savchenko seeing a landscape and a woman's portrait at an exhibition. He had thought them unusual, and had resolved to find[6] the unknown artist. For a long time he had stood in their little room in front of the canvases without saying a word, with just a faint smile on his face. Then he had uttered the very word which had often escaped[7] Glasha's lips—magnificent! He had come again. He had asked permission to bring other people round. And now on Sundays the Saburovs' room was filled with enthusiastic visitors. Saburov was glad of[8] the guests and willingly started up[9] long conversations with them, but his attitude towards their praises was restrained,[10] and he would reply—'you know I don't care for this thing. I began all right and then I made a mess of it'[11]—or else 'I didn't manage to get the light[12] properly, you see'. The man combined[13] great modesty with a belief in[14] the rightness of the path he had chosen. He believed that real painting would always get across, and that there was no need for him to strive for[15] recognition, only to work.

*Adapted from* I. EHRENBURG

[1] Say 'that in the fate of Saburov there had taken place no changes'.

[2] заста́вленный + instr. Distinguish between заставля́ть (заста́вить) 'to cram', 'fill up', 'block up', and заставля́ть (заста́вить) 'to force', 'compel'.

3 Invert the order, starting with 'basis' in the instr.

4 многое переменилось в жизни.

5 началось всё с того, что . . .

6 'To find' meaning 'to succeed in tracking down', as opposed to 'finding without necessarily looking' is разыскать. Its perfective form разыскивать means 'to try and find', 'to look for'. See *R.S.* 226, and N.B. the synonymous verb отыскивать (отыскать).

7 которое часто вырывалось у . . .

8 *R.S.* 45, and N.B. the verb радоваться.

9 Notice заводить (завести) and the main idioms associated with it: — разговор 'start up a conversation'; — граммофон 'turn on a gramophone'; — дружбу 'strike up a friendship'; — часы 'wind up a watch'; — мотор 'switch on an engine'; — будильник 'set an alarm-clock'.

10 он относился сдержанно к . . .

11 напортил: a rather colloquial perfective verb, literally 'did a lot of damage to'. Cf. some similar verbs in *R.S.* 240.

12 Say 'to convey', 'render': передавать (передать). 'To get across' in the final sentence will be доходить (дойти) до.

13 Say 'there was in the man great modesty combined with . . .'.

14 *R.S.* 41 (i).

15 *R.S.* 32 (i).

## 23

After secretly slipping the laudanum into your brandy-and-water, he wished you good-night, and went into his own room. Your rooms were linked by a communicating door.[1] On entering his own room, Mr. Godfrey (as he supposed) closed this door. His money troubles[2] kept him awake.[3] He sat in his dressing-gown and slippers, for nearly an hour, thinking over his position. Just as he was preparing to get into bed, he heard you, talking to yourself,[4] in your own room, and going to the door found that he had not shut it as he supposed.

He looked into[5] your room to see what was the matter. He discovered you with the candle in your hand just leaving[6] your bed-room. He heard you say to yourself, in a voice quite unlike your own voice, 'How[7] do I know? The Indians[8] may be hidden in the house'. It now occurred to him that the laudanum had taken some effect on you, which had not been foreseen by the doctor any more than by himself. Fearing that[9] an accident might happen, he followed you softly to see what you would do.

He followed you to Miss Verinder's sitting-room, and saw you go in. You left the door open. He looked through the crevice between the door and the post before he ventured into the room himself.[10]

WILKIE COLLINS

[1] сообща́лись две́рью. [2] Say 'difficulties'.
[3] Say 'did not for a long time allow him to fall asleep' ('allow' — дава́ть). [4] сама́ с собо́й.
[5] загляну́л в. Notice a similar use of the prefix за- in забра́ться 'to break in' (of burglars). Notice also я загляну́ в газе́ту 'I'll take a look at the newspaper'; ещё мо́гут загляну́ть покупа́тели 'customers might still look in'. [6] выходя́щим (instr.). [7] почём.
[8] Distinguish between инду́сы and инде́йцы.
[9] *R.S.* 265. Say 'something might happen', paying attention to the case of the pronoun что́-нибудь. [10] самому́.

## 24

Before you left the sitting-room again, you hesitated a little. Mr. Godfrey took advantage of this hesitation to get back again into his bed-room before you came out[1] and discovered[1] him. He had barely got back before[2] you got back too. You saw him (as he supposes) just as[3] he was passing through the door. At any rate you called to him in a strange, drowsy voice.

He came back to you. You looked at him in a dull, sleepy way.[4] You put the diamond into his hand. You said to him, 'Take it back, Godfrey, to your father's bank. It's safe[5] there—it's not safe here!' You turned away unsteadily, and put on your dressing-gown. You sat down in the large arm-chair in[6] your room. You said, 'I can't take it back to the bank. My head's like lead—and I can't feel my feet under me.'[7] Your head sank on the back of your chair—you heaved a heavy sigh—and you fell asleep.

Mr. Godfrey Ablewhite went back with the diamond into his own room. His statement is that he came to no conclusion at that time—except[8] that he would wait, and see what happened in the morning.

When the morning came, your language and actions showed that you were absolutely ignorant of what you had said and done overnight. At the same time, Miss Verinder's language and actions showed that she, in[9] mercy to you, was resolved to say nothing. If Mr. Godfrey Ablewhite chose[10] to keep the diamond, he might do so with perfect impunity. The Moonstone stood between him and[11] ruin. He put the Moonstone into his pocket.

WILKIE COLLINS

[1] Tense? Look at these actions from Godfrey's point of view.
[2] *R.S.* 391 (ii). [3] и́менно в то вре́мя, когда́.
[4] Use взгля́д. [5] Say 'in safety'.
[6] Insert a verb after 'arm-chair'.
[7] Say 'my legs do not support me at all'.
[8] кро́ме того. [9] Say 'out of'.
[10] Say 'saw fit', заблагорассу́дится + dat.. This word is only used in the 3rd singular present and neuter past.
[11] Say 'was saving him from'.

## 25

Simon got to bed at half-past four. At ten minutes past eight the telephone by[1] his bed was ringing.[2]

'Mr. Lent? This is Sir James Macrae's secretary speaking.[3] Sir James' car will call for you at half-past eight to[4] take you to the studio.'

'I shan't be ready[5] as soon as that, I'm afraid.'

There was a shocked pause;[6] then, the secretary said: 'Very well, Mr. Lent. I will see if some alternative arrangement[7] is possible and ring you in a few minutes.'

In the intervening time Simon fell asleep again. Then the bell woke him once more and the same impersonal voice addressed him.

'Mr. Lent? I have spoken to Sir James. His car will call for you at eight forty-five.'

Simon dressed hastily. Mrs. Shaw had not yet arrived,[8] so there was no breakfast for him. He found some stale cake in the kitchen cupboard and was eating it when Sir James' car arrived. He took a slice down with him, still munching.

'You needn't have brought[9] that,' said a severe voice from inside[10] the car. 'Sir James has sent you some breakfast. Get in quickly; we're late.'

In the corner, huddled in[11] rugs, sat a young woman in a jaunty[12] red hat; she had bright eyes and a very firm mouth.[13]

'I expect that you are Miss Harper.'

'No, I'm Elfreda Grits. We're working together on this film, I believe. I've been up all night[14] with Sir James. If you don't mind I'll go to sleep for[15] twenty minutes. You'll find a thermos of cocoa and some rabbit pie in the basket on the floor.'

'Does Sir James live on[16] cocoa and rabbit pie?'

'No; those are the remains of his supper. Please don't talk. I want to sleep.'

EVELYN WAUGH

[1] *R.S.* 563 (ii). [2] i.e. 'began to ring'. *R.S.* 233.

[3] Omit 'This is' and invert subject and verb.

[4] Say 'and will take' (отвезёт).

[5] я не успе́ю собра́ться. Собира́ться (собра́ться) is commonly used in the sense of preparing for a journey.

[6] возмущённое молча́ние.

[7] Say 'if it is possible to arrange the matter in some other way'.

[8] *R.S.* 208.

[9] Use an impersonal construction with an imperfective infinitive.

[10] из глубины́. [11] Say 'having wrapped herself into'.

[12] наря́дный or шика́рный are probably the best words here. Щегольско́й is more commonly used of men's than women's clothing, cf. English 'dandified'.

[13] Use гу́бы for 'mouth' and ре́зко оче́рченные for 'firm'.

[14] *R.S.* 243. [15] я посплю́ (сосну́) на.

[16] *R.S.* 671 (ii).

# 26

After that I met Wilson several times, either in the Piazza or on the beach. He was amiable and polite. He was always pleased to have a talk and I found out that he not only knew every inch[1] of the island but also the adjacent mainland.[2] He had read a great deal on all sorts of subjects, but his speciality was the history of Rome and on this he was very well informed.[3] He seemed to have little imagination and to be of no more than the average intelligence.[4] A commonplace man. I did not forget the odd remark he had made during the first short chat we had had by ourselves, but he never so much as approached the topic again.[5] One day on our return from the beach, dismissing[6] the cab at the Piazza, my friend and I told the driver to be ready to take us[7] to Anacapri at five. We were going to climb Monte Solaro, dine at a tavern we favoured, and walk down in the moonlight. For it was full moon and the views by night were lovely. Wilson was standing by and I asked him if he would care to join us.

'I'll come with pleasure,' he said.

But when the time came to set out my friend was not feeling well, he thought he had stayed too long in the water, and could not face[8] the long and tiring walk. So I went alone with Wilson. We climbed the mountain, admired the view,[9] and got back to the inn as night was falling, hungry and thirsty.[10]

W. SOMERSET MAUGHAM

1 Translate literally.

2 Here матери́к 'continent' would be inappropriate. Use земля́ or бéрег, e.g. близлежа́щий бéрег (N.B. 'adjacent' here means 'nearby', not 'touching').

3 осведомлён в + prep.

4 и лишь са́мые зауря́дные у́мственные спосо́бности (if у него́ and a nominative subject is used in the first part of the sentence).

5 'Never so much as', &c., will have to be rendered by some such paraphrase as он да́же никогда́ бо́льше не пыта́лся верну́ться.

[6] Say 'having returned and having settled up with' (расплати́вшись с + instr.). [7] быть гото́вым отвезти́ нас.
[8] не мог да́же поду́мать о . . . [9] *R.S.* 47.
[10] In the absence of a single adjective for 'thirsty' it is best to translate the end of this sentence by using two nouns (e.g. го́лодом и жа́ждой) dependent on some such word as томи́мые.

## 27

Christmas came.

Paul awoke before dawn. Christmas Eve was a double festival for him, because it coincided with his birthday. One can imagine how impatiently the boy had looked forward to[1] the arrival of this joyful but altogether strange day when all at once he became four. Three only yesterday,[2] but four today, whenever can[3] it happen? During the night, most likely.

Paul had long ago decided to watch out for[4] this mysterious moment when children become one year older.[5] Awaking in the middle of the night, he opened his eyes wide but did not notice anything out of the ordinary. Everything was as usual: the chest of drawers, the wardrobe, his rocking horse. How old is he now, three or four?

Paul began to examine his arms closely and jerked[6] his legs once or twice under the blanket. No, his arms and legs were just as they had been the night before, when he was getting into bed. But maybe his head had grown a little?[7] He carefully felt his head, his cheeks, his nose, his ears. They all seemed the same as[8] the day before. How strange! Stranger still,[9] because in the morning he will certainly be four. How old is he now, then? It would be a good idea to awaken daddy. He's bound to know. But the thought of scrambling from beneath the warm blanket and tramping[10] barefoot over the floor—no thank you![11] Best just to pretend to be asleep and wait for the transformation with your eyes shut.

*Translated and adapted from* VALENTIN KATAEV

[1] дожида́лся (imperfective aspect because the sense is continuous).
[2] вот то́лько ещё вчера́ бы́ло три.
[3] The meaning here is 'has it time to?' [4] подстере́чь.
[5] *R.S.* 650.
[6] The verb used here is подры́гать (see *R.S.* 51 and 231) which is used pre-eminently of jerking the legs.
[7] The verb used here is выраста́ть (вы́расти). This verb emphasizes growing bigger, whereas расти́ refers to the process of growth: cf. трава́ растёт, *but* за э́то вре́мя трава́ успе́ла значи́тельно вы́расти: 'The grass is growing', *but* 'the grass during this time had grown a great deal'. Вы́расти may also mean 'to grow up' (в промы́шленном го́роде). Notice also the verb отраста́ть (отрасти́) which means 'to grow after being cut' (of hair, a beard, nails).
[8] как бу́дто бы те же, что. [9] *R.S.* 394 (v). [10] шлёпать.
[11] нет уж спаси́бо. Уж is used here as a strengthening particle.

## 28

Peter's[1] moment of greatest triumph and happiness had arrived.[2] It was not yet one o'clock[3] but he had already run round all his friends in the house, showing them his brand-new grammar school cap and excitedly telling them that he had just sat[4] an examination.

There was, in all conscience, almost nothing[5] to tell. Properly speaking, there had been no examination at all, only a simple entrance test lasting fifteen minutes. It had begun at half-past ten, and at five past eleven the assistant in the shop next door to the grammar school handed the boy his old straw hat, wrapped up in[6] paper. Peter put on his cap before the mirror in the shop and did not take it off[7] until[8] the evening.

'What a smart job I made of that examination!'[9] he said excitedly to himself as he hurried home along the street. He peeped into every shop window, just to have another look[10] at himself in his cap.

'Calm down, my boy,' said his aunt, her chin quivering with laughter. 'That was no[11] examination, only an entrance test.'

'Oh, auntie, how can you say such a thing?' shouted Peter so that the whole street could hear;[12] flushed[13] with anger, he stamped[14] his feet and was ready to burst into tears of resentment. 'Why, you didn't even see it, you sat in the waiting-room the whole time and you have no right to speak. I tell you, it *was* an examination.'

*Translated and adapted from* VALENTIN KATAEV

[1] *R.S.* 147. [2] Word order. *R.S.* 773.

[3] час дня 'one o'clock in the afternoon'. час но́чи 'one o'clock in the morning'.

[4] The verb used here is экзаменова́лся. Alternatives are держа́ть or сдава́ть (сдать) экза́мен. The verb выде́рживать (вы́держать) means 'to pass an examination'. The perfective verb сдать, when used with a suitable adverb, may also mean 'to pass': он блиста́тельно сдал матема́тику 'he passed brilliantly in mathematics'.

[5] *R.S.* 300.

[6] в followed by acc., cf. она́ была́ оде́та в шерстяно́й костю́м 'she was dressed in a woollen costume'. [7] *R.S.* 308. [8] до самого́.

[9] уж, как я ло́вко вы́держал экза́мен: cf. note 4 above.

[10] Use уви́деть and see *R.S.* 258.

[11] Word order. The emphasis of the English 'no' can be expressed in Russian by placing не immediately before the word it qualifies.

[12] на всю у́лицу. [13] Say 'turning purple with'. [14] *R.S.* 51.

## 29

For some reason I hesitated.

'He says so,' I replied cautiously. 'At any rate, he is much better.'[1]

'Yes, I can see that; but he is still in a very nervous condition.'

'Ah!' I said, 'that is only—only at certain times.'

As we went together from room to room,[2] I forgot everything except the fact of[3] her presence. I began gloomily to speculate on the chances of her ultimately marrying Alresca,[4] and a remark from her[5] awoke me from my abstraction. We were nearing the top of the house.

'It is all familiar to me, in a way,'[6] she said.

'Why, you said the same downstairs. Have you been here before?'

'Never, to my knowledge.'

We were traversing a long, broad passage, side by side. Suddenly I tripped over an unexpected single stair, and nearly fell.[7] Rosa, however, had allowed for it.[8]

'I didn't see that step,' I said.

'Nor I,'[9] she answered, 'but I knew, somehow, that it was there. It is very strange and uncanny, and I shall insist on[10] an explanation from Alresca.' She gave a forced[11] laugh.

As I fumbled with[12] the handle of the door she took hold of my hand.

'Listen!' she said excitedly, 'this will be a small room, and over the mantelpiece is a little round picture of[13] a dog.'

ARNOLD BENNETT

[1] *R.S.* 308.

[2] переходи́ть из ко́мнаты в ко́мнату or проходи́ть по ко́мнатам.

[3] Omit 'the fact of'.

[4] Say 'to reflect that she would probably ultimately marry'. Translate 'that' о том, что.

[5] Say 'her remark'.

[6] как бу́дто.

[7] *R.S.* 207.

[8] ступи́ла на неё, бу́дто зна́ла.

[9] я то́же.

[10] обяза́тельно потре́бую.

[11] принуждённо.

[12] Say' sought gropingly'.

[13] Say 'depicting'.

## 30

There is no need for me to speak of the novels I wrote during the next[1] few years. One of them, *Mrs. Craddock*, was not unsuccessful and I have reprinted[2] it in the collected editions of my works. Of the others, two were novelisations[3] of plays that I had failed to get produced[4] and for long they lay on my conscience like a discreditable action; I would have given much to suppress[5] them. But I know now that my qualms were unnecessary. Even the greatest authors have written a number of very poor books. Balzac himself[6] left a good many out of the Comédie Humaine, and of those he inserted there are several[7] that only the student troubles to read; the writer can rest assured that the books he would like to forget will be forgotten. I wrote one of these books because I had to have enough money to carry me on for[8] the following year; the other because I was at the time much taken with a young person of extravagant tastes and the gratification of my desires was frustrated by the attentions of more opulent admirers who were able to provide the luxuries[9] that her frivolous soul[10] hankered after. I had nothing much to offer but a serious disposition and a sense of humour. I determined to write a book that would enable me to earn three or four hundred pounds with which I could hold my own[11] with my rivals. For[12] the young person was attractive.

W. SOMERSET MAUGHAM

[1] Use послéдующий which normally translates English 'subsequent' and therefore 'next' when, as here, it qualifies a plural noun: cf. егó послéдующие сочинéния 'his subsequent works'. Compare below 'the following year'.

[2] Say 'included'.

[3] The word романизáция means 'romanization', e.g. романизáция гáллов. Use here the noun переработка or the past participle passive of переработать.

[4] Often in Russian such expressions are best translated by using the main verb alone. *R.S.* 259. Say 'which I failed to put on'.

[5] 'To suppress' of a newspaper is запрещáть (запретúть). Here use изъя́ть из продáжи.

[6] *R.S.* 519.

[7] Do not attempt to translate 'there are'. Recast the English to read 'and only students trouble to read several of those which . . .' ('to take the trouble to' считáть себя́ обя́занным).

[8] Say 'to live through'. *R.S.* 243.

[9] The word рóскошь exists only in the singular. 'Luxuries' предмéты рóскоши: cf. above 'of extravagant tastes' со вкýсом к рóскоши.

[10] Say 'her frivolous nature'.

[11] Use the expression постáвить на рáвную нóгу с.

[12] и́бо.

# 31

After a while,[1] finding that[2] nothing more happened, she decided on going into the garden once more; but, alas for poor Alice, when she got to[3] the door, she found[2] she had forgotten the little golden key, and when she went back to the table for it, she found she could not possibly reach it. She could see quite plainly through the glass, and she tried her best to climb up one of the legs of the table,[4] but it was too slippery, and when she had tired herself out with trying,[5] the poor little thing sat down and cried.

'Come, there's no use in crying like that!'[6] said Alice to herself rather sharply; 'I advise you to leave off this minute!' She generally gave herself very good advice[7] (though she very seldom followed it), and sometimes she scolded herself[8] so severely[9] as to bring tears[10] into her eyes, and once she remembered trying to box her own ears for having cheated herself[8] in a game of croquet she was playing against herself;[11] for this curious child was very fond of pretending to be two people.[12] 'But it's no use now,' thought poor Alice, 'to pretend to be two people! Why, there's hardly enough of me left to make[13] *one* respectable person!'

LEWIS CARROLL

[1] че́рез or спустя́, not по́сле.

[2] находя́, что would not be idiomatic Russian, nor would она́ нашла́, что забы́ла. Находи́ть (найти́) followed by что and a clause normally suggests the rather stronger English 'come to the conclusion that'. Translate by ви́дя, что and она́ уви́дела, что; or use the verb замеча́ть (заме́тить).

[3] подойдя́ к. See *R.S.* 319 for common examples of gerunds in -а (-я) from perfective verbs.

[4] *R.S.* 59.

[5] измýчив себя́ попы́тками.

[6] Use the impersonal expression ну, бу́дет and the infinitive.

[7] Use сове́т in the plural.

[8] Separate брани́ть and себя́. Брани́ться means 'to quarrel' or

'abuse each other'. Similarly below, обману́ть себя́ not обману́ться which means 'to be deceived'. [9] си́льно.

[10] Say 'that tears came into' (выступа́ли на+prep.).

[11] Say 'with herself'.

[12] люби́ла представля́ть из себя́ двух люде́й.

[13] едва́ ли хва́тит меня́ на + acc. *R.S.* 302. The tense of the verb indicates the English implied future.

## 32

'By the way,' said Dr. Ansell one evening when Morel was in Sheffield, 'we've got[1] a man in the fever hospital[2] here who comes from Nottingham—Dawes. He doesn't seem to have many belongings[3] in this world.'

'Baxter Dawes!' Paul exclaimed.

'That's the man—has been a fine fellow, physically, I should think. Been in a bit of a mess lately.[4] You know him?'

'He used to work at the place where I am.'

'Did he?[5] Do you know anything about him? He's just sulking, or he'd[6] be a lot better than he is by now.'

'I don't know anything of his home circumstances, except that he's separated from his wife and has been a bit down,[7] I believe. But tell him about me, will you? Tell him I'll come and see him.'

The next time Morel saw the doctor he said:

'And what about Dawes?'[8]

'I said to him,' answered the other, ' "Do you know a man from Nottingham named Morel?" and he looked at me as if he'd jump at my throat.[9] So I said,[10] "I see you know the name; it's Paul Morel." Then I told him about your saying you would go and see him. "What does he want?" he said, as if you were a policeman.'

'And did he say he would see me?' asked Paul.

'He wouldn't say anything—good, bad or indifferent,'[11] replied the doctor.

'Why not?'

'That's what I want to know. There he lies and sulks, day in, day out.[12] Can't get a word of information out of him.'[13]

'Do you think I might go?'[14] asked Paul.

'You might.'

D. H. LAWRENCE

[1] у нас лежи́т. *R.S.* 328 (ii).

[2] больни́ца для зара́зных больны́х.

[3] пожи́тки. Cf. принадле́жности in the plural, which is normally combined with an epithet in the general meaning of 'tackle', 'outfit', 'things', &c.: бри́твенные принадле́жности 'shaving things'.

[4] The meaning here may be simply был в беде́ (cf. попа́сть в беду́) or more likely that of 'moral or physical degeneration' развинти́лся.

[5] вот как? 'really?', 'indeed?', 'is that so?'

[6] а то. *R.S.* 405.

[7] Perhaps немно́го угнетён. Cf. быть в угнетённом состоя́нии 'to be in low spirits'.

[8] что же Доус?

[9] Say 'seize me by the throat'.

[10] Russian frequently uses the present tense in this context, where in English the corresponding 'so I says to him' would be regional and ungrammatical. Notice the intensifying particle: я ему́ и говорю́.

[11] ни да, ни нет, ни что ему́ всё равно́.

[12] *R.S.* 553 (iii).

[13] не могу́ доби́ться от него́ хоть сло́ва о нём са́мом. See *R.S.* 32. Alternatively вы́давить из него́, which is a shade stronger.

[14] пойти́ мне к нему́?

## 33

'Has M. Vigot been to see you?' Phuong asked.

'Yes. He left a quarter of an hour ago. Was the film good?' She had already laid out the tray[1] in the bedroom and now she was lighting the lamp.

'It was very sad,' she said, 'but the colours were lovely. What did M. Vigot want?'

'He wanted to ask me some questions.'

'What about?'

'This and that.[2] I don't think he will bother me again.'[3]

'I like films with happy endings[4] best,' Phuong said. 'Are you ready to smoke?'

'Yes.' I lay down on the bed and Phuong set to work with her needle.[5] She said, 'They cut off the girl's head.'[6]

'What a strange thing to do.'

'It was in the French Revolution.'

'Oh. Historical. I see.'

'It was very sad all the same.'

'I can't worry much about people in history.'

'And her lover—he went back to his garret—and he was miserable and he wrote a song—you see, he was a poet, and soon all the people who had cut off the head of his girl were singing his song.[7] It was the Marseillaise.'

'It doesn't sound very historical,'[8] I said.

'He stood there at the edge[9] of the crowd while they were singing, and he looked very bitter and when he smiled you knew he was even more bitter and that he was thinking of her. I cried a lot and so did my sister.'

'Your sister? I can't believe it.'[10]

'She is very sensitive. That horrid man Granger was there. He was drunk and he kept on laughing. But it was not funny at all. It was sad.'

GRAHAM GREENE

[1] Translate by 'got ready' приготóвила. [2] *R.S.* 461 (i).

[3] Here, after the negative antecedent, the subjunctive would be usual, but not obligatory: я не дýмаю, чтóбы он стал меня́ ещё беспокóить. *R.S.* 267.

[4] Each film has one ending: use the singular.

[5] принялáсь орýдовать иглóй. Notice the expressions in which орýдовать is associated with an instrument in the meaning 'to put to its proper use', 'handle', 'manage', 'ply', 'wield' (топорóм, ножóм, &c.), орýдовать всем 'to run the show'.

[6] With отрубáть (отруби́ть) use the dative of the person ('to cut off to the girl the head').

[7] Use распевáть (распéть), meaning 'to spend one's time singing' or 'to sing through'. It is a useful verb if a present gerund (which петь lacks) is required.

[8] In the absence of a suitable adverb to use with звучи́т, one might

translate что́-то не о́чень похо́же на исто́рию, where что́-то suggests 'it looks as if'; or with a negative verb 'I rather doubt if': что́-то не по́мню 'I doubt if I can remember'.

[9] на краю́ would not be used of a crowd (it would be of something with a definite edge, such as a town), but с кра́ю толпы́ (N.B. the stress) is possible.

[10] There is an opportunity here to use the perfective future to express impossibility: вот не пове́рю. *R.S.* 269. Alternatively the impersonal expression что-то не ве́рится is possible.

## 34

I told her, 'Pyle's coming at six.'

'I will go and see[1] my sister,' she said.

'I expect he'd like to see you.'

'He does not like me or my family. When you were away[2] he did not come once to my sister, although she had invited him. She was very hurt.'

'You needn't[3] go out.'

'If he wanted to see me, he would have asked us to the Majestic. He wants to talk to you privately[4]—about business.'

'What is his business?'

'People say he imports a great many things.'

'What things?'

'Drugs, medicines . . .'

'Those are for the trachoma teams[5] in the north.'

'Perhaps. The Customs must not open them.[6] They are diplomatic parcels. But once there was a mistake—the man was discharged. The First Secretary threatened[7] to stop all imports.'[8]

'What was in the case?'

'Plastic.'

I said idly, 'What did they want plastic for?'[9]

When Phuong had gone, I wrote home. A man from Reuter's was leaving for[10] Hong Kong in a few days and he could mail my letter from there. I knew my appeal was hopeless, but I was not going to reproach myself later for not taking every possible measure. I wrote to the Managing Editor that this was[11] the wrong moment to change their correspondent. General de Lattre was[11] dying in Paris: the French were about to[11] withdraw altogether from Hoa Binh: the north had never been in greater danger. I wasn't suitable, I told him, for a foreign editor[12]—I was a reporter, I had[11] no real opinions about anything.

GRAHAM GREENE

[1] An opportunity to use схожу́ *R.S.* 287 (ii).

[2] когда́ тебя́ не́ было.

[3] тебе́ не́зачем *R.S.* 300.

[4] Note the stress on с глазу на́ глаз, an idiomatic alternative to наедине́.

[5] отря́ды по борьбе́ с трахо́мой.

[6] The meaning is that they are not allowed to: say 'at the Customs it is forbidden to open them' (the imperfective infinitive in Russian, to denote a general rule). Вскрыва́ть (вскрыть) is the verb normally used of opening letters, parcels, &c., at the Customs (it also has the special meaning of 'to dissect' or 'conduct a post-mortem').

[7] In the context of the novel, the reference is to the American Embassy and its threat not to import anything more: пригрози́л, что америка́нцы бо́льше ничего́ сюда́ не бу́дут ввози́ть. Грози́ть and угрожа́ть are both imperfective verbs which can mean 'to threaten to do something' (infinitive), 'to threaten that you will do something' (что + the indicative), and 'to threaten somebody with something' (instr.). Пригрози́ть is the normal perfective; погрози́ть the perfective commonly used to mean 'to make a threatening gesture'. See *R.S.* 47 (ii) and, for the other use of грози́ть where the threatened misfortune is the subject, *R.S.* 41.

[8] Note that the noun ввоз denotes the action of importing and has no plural (in the singular it can also mean, collectively, the total amount of imports). 'Imports' meaning 'the goods imported' are вво́зные (и́мпортные) това́ры.

[9] заче́м им пластма́сса? 'Idly' may be rendered рассе́янно.

[10] собира́лся в.

[11] Keep the tenses of direct speech.

[12] я не гожу́сь на роль заве́дующего иностра́нным отде́лом. Cf. он никуда́ не годи́тся 'he is no use for anything'.

## 35

For nearly all readers[1] everywhere (even in Russia itself) Russian literature begins in[2] the nineteenth century. It is the youngest literature in Europe, and it opened with what has been called 'The Golden Age of Russian Poetry' and the publication[3] of Pushkin's first book of verse in 1820. Pushkin is to the Russians what Dante is to Italians and Goethe to Germans.[4] And as the English may sometimes speak of Shakespeare and Milton together, but without intending either to compare them or assert their equality, so for many years Russians coupled with Pushkin's name that of Lermontov.

This 'Golden Age' soon ended. It was followed by the era of the great Russian novelists, which was of far more importance to the world at large;[5] for poetry—and this is most apt to be true of[6] the best—may be impossible to translate. In 1837 Pushkin was killed in a duel at the age of 35; and this catastrophe was, as we shall see, a turning-point in the career of the younger poet, Lermontov. He also was killed in a duel, and when he was only 27.

Lermontov was born in Moscow in 1814. He was the son of a poor army officer who was descended from[7] a Scot, one George Learmont, who in 1613 had entered first the Polish then the Russian army as a soldier of fortune.[8] His father had made a runaway match with[9] a romantic girl belonging to a wealthy landed family. His mother died in the third year of a probably not very happy marriage, and her aristocratic mother[10] adopted the future poet. Afterwards she did all in her power to alienate him from his father, whom he adored.

DESMOND MACCARTHY

[1] Say 'reading public'.

[2] *R.S.* 685 (i).

[3] One might say 'when, in 1820, appeared'. Note that the expression вы́йти из печа́ти means 'to appear in print' and not 'to go out of print'.

[4] Follow the English construction.

[5] In the context it is probably best to say 'for the world abroad'. Also possible is 'for the whole world', but this, of course, would include Russia.

[6] Say simply 'especially the best'.

[7] Use a noun in apposition, 'the descendant of'.

[8] 'Mercenaries' in Russian is наёмные войска́.

[9] Introduce a Russian clause meaning 'who ran away with him in secret', using a participial construction. Note that in the meaning of 'to run away' бежáть is both imperfective and perfective.

[10] Say 'mother-aristocrat'.

## 36

When I came back to the front we still lived in that town. There were many more guns in the country around and the spring had come.[1] The fields were green[2] and there were small green shoots on the vines, the trees along the road had small leaves and a breeze came from the sea.[3] I saw the town with the hill and the old castle above it in a cup[4] in the hills with the mountains beyond,[5] brown mountains with a little green[6] on their slopes. In the town there were more guns, there were some new hospitals, you met British men and sometimes women, on the street, and a few more houses had been hit by shell fire.[7] It was warm and like the spring[8] and I walked down the alleyway of trees, warmed from the sun on the wall,[9] and found[10] we still lived in the same house and that it all looked the same[11] as when I had left it. The door was open, there was a soldier sitting on a bench outside[12] in the sun, an ambulance was waiting by the side door and inside the door,[13] as I went in,[14] there was the smell of[15] marble floors and hospital. It was all as I had left it[16] except that now it was spring. I looked in the door of[17] the big room and saw the major sitting at his desk,[18] the window open and the sunlight coming into the room. He did not see me and I did not know whether to go in and report[19] or go upstairs first and clean up. I decided to go on upstairs.

[1] Word order. *R.S.* 773.

[2] Use the verb which means both 'to grow green' and 'to show green'.

[3] Word order. Say 'on the vines were . . . on the trees were . . . from the sea blew'. The verbs 'were' and 'had' may here be rendered by

some such verbs as показа́лись and раскры́лись, to avoid the use of бы́ли in successive phrases. [4] In this sense котлови́на.

[5] Begin a new sentence: 'Beyond were the mountains . . .'.

[6] Say 'barely showing green' едва́ зелене́ющие.

[7] проби́ты снаря́дами. [8] Say 'as in spring'.

[9] If алле́я is used as the antecedent (вдоль по алле́е), the sentence might continue: согре́той со́лнцем, припека́вшим сте́ну 'which baked the wall'. A verb is needed here in Russian (not just на стене́).

[10] Not нашёл.

[11] *R.S.* 340 'to look like'. Remember to use the present tense.

[12] Use снару́жи, not на дворе́, to avoid the sequence на скамье́, на дворе́, на со́лнце. Гре́ясь may also be inserted.

[13] Say simply 'inside'. [14] когда́. *R.S.* 375 (ii).

[15] *R.S.* 49.

[16] как при моём отъе́зде (ухо́де). See also *R.S.* 527.

[17] я заглянýл в дверь (веду́щую) в . . ., i.e. the door leading *into*.

[18] To avoid a series of instrumental participles after увидел, break the sentence up by putting a semi-colon after 'desk', and continuing with two verbs: 'the window was open and the sunlight was coming into the room'.

[19] я не знал, войти́ ли и доложи́ть (заяви́ть) о своём прибы́тии. For the use of the Russian infinitive to express 'should', 'ought to', see *R.S.* 275.

## 37

This is how we parted. As we stood outside his hotel one night, he said, looking up at the sky: 'I hope it will be fine to-morrow. I am leaving for England in the morning.'

'You're not serious.'[1]

'Perfectly. I have to get back. I've some work[2] to do that I can't manage here.'

'But—but have you made all your preparations?'

'Preparations?' He almost grinned.[3] 'I've none to make.'[4]

'But—enfin, Dick, England is not the other side of the boulevard.'[5]

'It isn't much farther off,' said he. 'Only a few hours, you know.' The door cracked open.[6]

'Ah, I wish I'd known at the beginning of the evening.'

I felt hurt.[7] I felt as a woman must feel when a man takes out his watch and remembers[8] an appointment that cannot possibly concern her, except that its claim is the stronger.[9] 'Why didn't you tell me?'

He put out his hand and stood, lightly swaying[10] upon the step as though the whole hotel were his ship, and the anchor weighed.

'I forgot. Truly I did. But you'll write,[11] won't you? Good night, old chap. I'll be over again one of these days.'[12]

KATHERINE MANSFIELD

[1] Say 'You're joking' and follow with 'Not at all'.
[2] кóе-какáя рабóта. Omit 'to do'.
[3] Say 'He could scarcely suppress a smile'.
[4] мне нéчего собирáться.
[5] Say, for example, 'going to England is not the same thing as crossing the street', using infinitives in Russian.
[6] Say 'opened with a crack'.
[7] Use such an expression as is described in *R.S.* 309.
[8] Say 'looks at his watch and remembers'. Here the two actions form one whole. *R.S.* 323.
[9] Say 'not concerning her at all but demanding his attention more than she'.
[10] The verb покáчиваться means 'to rock' or 'to sway' slightly.
[11] Is only one action envisaged?
[12] на-днях́ may mean either 'the other day' or 'one of these days'.

## 38

The train rumbled across[1] Germany in the last week of March. Lenin was silent; but his fellow-travellers talked cheerful nonsense and ate larger meals than they had been accustomed to,[2] whilst a small boy filled the whole carriage with his noise.[3] They looked out of the windows at the German fields and noticed that there were few men about; and when they were shunted[4] at Berlin, some German Socialists appeared. Then they were on the Baltic steamer; and when they got to Stockholm, someone made a speech. But

Sweden was behind them now, and they were driving into Finland over the ice at Torneå. This was Russian territory at last, and they saw again the familiar[5] uniforms and the dilapidated rolling-stock they knew so well.[5] The small boy was playing with a Russian soldier; and as the little stations of the north went by, one of the party hung out of the window to shout, 'Long live the world revolution'; but no one on the platform seemed to care. Lenin was arguing about the war with someone in a carriage full of soldiers, who stood on the seats to listen to[6] the argument. His face was white and strained; for Petrograd was coming nearer, and they could not tell what Petrograd might hold.[7]

PHILIP GUEDALLA

[1] Say 'crossed rumbling'. [2] Say 'ate more than usual'.
[3] пронзи́тельно крича́л на весь ваго́н. Cf. Passage 28, note 12.
[4] Use маневри́ровать intransitively.
[5] Say, for example, 'the uniforms and dilapidated rolling-stock—everything so familiar'. [6] Cf. Passage 7, note 3.
[7] Say 'what awaited them there'. Be careful of the tense in Russian.

## 39

I feel that the time has come when I must endeavour to face facts.[1] Ten months ago I was a sane, strong, healthy man; now[2] I am weak, irresolute and, I fear, on the verge of going mad.

Perhaps I am only imagining things.[3] But if I set down[4] all that is happening here—or rather, that which I believe to be happening—when I look at[4] what I have written again next day, I shall at least know that I haven't dreamed[5] the whole horrible business overnight.

That is why I have decided to keep a journal. In it I intend not only to give an account of these strange experiences of which I have recently been the victim, but also to make an attempt to rationalize[6] them. If I can somehow argue matters out with myself[7] until I reach a logical conclusion as to what lies at the bottom of my fears, I shall, perhaps, be able to face them better and save my sanity.[8]

I used to enjoy writing essays, and the work involved in setting down my thoughts coherently should help a lot to keep my mind free from[9] aimless, agonizing dread of the night to come.[10] I shall not write in the evenings, however, since the accursed shadows in this big room often make me jumpy near sundown, and might lead me to exaggerate the facts. I'll work on it in the mornings, or afternoons, when the good, clear daylight, streaming in[11] through the broad windows, makes me feel more like the man[12] I used to be.

DENNIS WHEATLEY

[1] Say 'to look facts in the face', placing 'facts' in the dative case.

[2] Use the conjunction же to strengthen the contrast: 'now, however'.

[3] э́то то́лько игра́ воображе́ния.

[4] Future tense.

[5] 'To dream' may be translated either ви́деть во сне or by the impersonal expression приви́деться во сне. The verb мечта́ть means 'to day-dream'.

[6] Say 'to find a rational explanation for them' placing 'them' in the dative case.

[7] One possibility here is to use разобра́ться в 'to arrive at an understanding of', 'to get to the bottom of'. Replace 'until' by 'and'.

[8] душе́вное равнове́сие.

[9] The verb прогоня́ть (прогна́ть) can have the meaning of 'to keep at bay' unpleasant thoughts or emotions.

[10] Say 'which I feel at the thought of the approaching night'. *R.S.* 527.

[11] Say 'pours in streams' and continue 'and I feel'.

[12] Translate literally, following 'man' with a relative pronoun in the instrumental case. For 'the' see *R.S.* 468.

## 40

'Don't be cynical, Henry,' Mrs. Ford was saying, as[1] their car sped towards home.

'What's the good fooling yourself about[2] people?' asked Henry. 'They all have something to sell.'

'Most of those people have all the money they need, I am sure.'

'All the same, there's not one of them but[3] wants more, and would be glad to get it out of you or me. The first step is to get to know you.'

'Such thoughts poison human relationships, dear.'

'Well, I never put on glad rags and went out unless[4] I was after something, and my guess is it's the same with them.'

'The dancing was beautiful.'

'It was all right. But I'll bet they're dancing jazz right now.'

The chauffeur and the guard were cut off from this conversation by a glass partition in the car.[5] They kept their eyes fixed on the road ahead.[6] Passing a stretch of vacant land, they saw through the rain[7] a woman coming towards the road. She appeared to be staggering,[8] and as they came near she began waving, and running faster, as if to intercept them. They had to swerve[9] to avoid[10] her. The second car, close behind, swerved also.

'What was that?' asked the chauffeur.

'Maybe she's drunk,' said the guard.

The car sped on.[11] They had their orders, they stopped for nothing. They were carrying a billion dollars, and such a sum of money cannot manifest either sympathy or curiosity; it has enough to do to take care of itself.[12]

Henry and his wife had not observed the episode. They were settled back in their seats, resting.[13] They were not so young as they had been.[14]

UPTON SINCLAIR

[1] Do not use как, but когда́ or в то вре́мя, как or пока́.

[2] относи́тельно. [3] все они́ до еди́ного 'they one and all'.

[4] Say 'whenever I . . . I was always . . .'.

[5] Say 'finding themselves on the other side of a glass partition, could not hear'. [6] Say 'They did not take their eyes off the road'.

[7] *R.S.* 613 (ii). [8] поша́тывалась. [9] кру́то поверну́ть.

[10] об'е́хать. [11] мча́лся да́льше.

[12] ей хвата́ет свои́х забо́т.

[13] Say 'They were resting, having settled back against the back of the seat'.

[14] го́ды уж бы́ли не те.

# 41

At length we are once more come to our hero; and, to say truth, we have been obliged to part with him so long,[1] that, considering the condition in which we left him, I apprehend many of our readers have concluded we intended to abandon him for ever; he being at present[2] in that situation in which prudent people usually desist from inquiring any farther after their friends, lest they should be shocked by hearing[3] such friends had hanged themselves.

But, in reality, if we have[4] not all the virtues, I will boldly say, neither[5] have[4] we all the vices of a prudent character, and though it is not easy to conceive circumstances much more miserable than those of poor Jones[6] at present, we shall return[7] to him, and attend upon[7] him with the same diligence as if he was wantoning[8] in the brightest beams of fortune.

Mr. Jones, then, and his companion Partridge, left the inn a few minutes after[9] the departure of Squire Western, and pursued the same road on foot, for the hostler told them that no horses were by any means to be at that time procured at Upton.[10] On they marched with heavy hearts;[11] for though their disquiet proceeded from very different reasons,[12] yet displeased they were both; and if Jones sighed bitterly, Partridge grunted altogether as sadly at every step.

HENRY FIELDING

[1] Say 'we were obliged to part with him so long ago'.

[2] This offers a good opportunity to use the common Russian conjunction ведь, which often corresponds to English 'for'. Say ведь он попа́л в то положе́ние.

[3] Say simply 'fearing to hear'.

[4] Use in Russian more precise words than 'have': e.g. 'cannot boast of', 'suffer from'.

[5] то́же.

[6] Use two nouns, 'the poor fellow Jones'.

[7] The nature of these two actions is different; one is completed in a moment, the other is durative. Express aspectivally.

[8] Say 'bathing in' and translate quite literally. Cf. купáться в зóлоте 'to be rolling in money'.

[9] *R.S.* 538.

[10] Recast the word-order in Russian. Say 'horses at that time, according to the hostler, it was impossible to procure in Upton for any money'. Remember in translating 'for any money' that the whole clause is negative.

[11] понýро.

[12] Say 'the reasons for (of) the disquiet of each were different'.

## 42

There were three of us children, Geoffrey my elder brother, myself, and my sister Mary, who was one year my junior,[1] the sweetest child and the most beautiful that I have ever known. We were very happy children, and our beauty was the pride of[2] our father and mother, and the envy of[2] other parents. I was the darkest of the three,[3] dark indeed to swarthiness, but in Mary the Spanish blood showed only in her rich eyes of velvet hue, and in the glow upon her cheek that was like the blush on a ripe fruit. My mother used to call me her little Spaniard, because of[4] my swarthiness, that is when my father was not near, for such names angered him. She never[5] learned to speak English very well, but he would suffer her to speak in no other tongue before[6] him. Still, when he was not there she spoke Spanish, of which language, however, I alone of the family became a master[7]—and that more because of certain volumes of old[8] Spanish romances which she had by her, than for any other reason.[9] From my earliest childhood I was fond of such tales, and it was by[10] promising that I should read them[11] that she persuaded me to learn Spanish. For my mother's heart still yearned towards her old sunny home, and often she would talk of it with us children, more especially in the winter season which she hated as I do. Once I asked her if she wished to go back to Spain. She shivered[12] and answered no, for there dwelt one who[13] was her enemy and would kill her; also her heart was with us children and our father.

H. RIDER HAGGARD

In this passage several long English sentences should be split up into shorter Russian sentences. This is often necessary in translating from English into Russian.

[1] Say 'one year younger than I'. *R.S.* 500.
[2] Use verbal constructions.
[3] *R.S.* 144 (vi).
[4] *R.S.* 619.
[5] 'Never', in this English use as a strong negative, without temporal meaning, is best translated into Russian by так и не. Sometimes 'never' is best left untranslated in Russian.
[6] *R.S.* 588.
[7] Re-cast this clause to read, 'but of all the children knew Spanish only I'. In a final position 'I' acquires an emphasis which is in keeping with the sense.
[8] стари́нные.
[9] Say, 'and even then (да и то) most probably because my mother had' (omit 'by her').
[10] Say 'my mother persuaded me to learn Spanish by promising' (тем, что обеща́ла).
[11] Say 'to give them to me to read'.
[12] *R.S.* 323.
[13] Meaning 'a certain man who'. *R.S.* 502.

## 43

Three nights later we set sail with a fair wind. I bade farewell to the far country where so many things had happened to me, and which according to my reckoning I had first sighted on this very day eighteen years before.[1]

Of my journey to Spain I have nothing of note to tell. It was[2] more prosperous than such voyages often are,[3] and within[4] ten weeks of the date of our lifting anchor at Vera Cruz, we let it drop in the harbour of Cadiz. Here I sojourned but two days, for as it chanced, there was[5] an English ship in the harbour, and in her I took a passage, although I was obliged to sell the smallest of the emeralds from the necklace to find the means to do so, the money that Marina gave me being spent.[6] This emerald sold for a great sum, however, with part of which I purchased clothing suitable[7] to a person of rank, taking the rest of the gold with me. I grieved to part with the stone indeed, but necessity knows no law.

On board the English ship they thought me a Spanish adventurer who had made money in the Indies, and I did not undeceive them, since I would be left to my own company for a while that I might prepare my mind to return to[8] ways of life that it had long forgotten. Therefore I sat apart like some proud don, saying little[9] but listening much,[9] and learning all I could of what had chanced in England since I left it some twenty years before.[10]

H. RIDER HAGGARD

[1] назáд.

[2] Use the verb протекáть followed by an appropriate adverb.

[3] Say 'than many such voyages'.

[4] Omit. Begin a new sentence 'Having lifted anchor . . . we ten weeks later dropped it'.

[5] *R.S.* 328.

[6] Use the verb вы́йти in its meaning of 'to run out'.

[7] The verb приодéться may mean 'to dress oneself' in the sense of 'acquiring clothing'. Follow with как подобáет, noting the present tense, although the whole passage is in the past tense.

[8] внýтренне подготóвиться к встрéче с.

[9] Work in помéньше, побóльше.

[10] Say 'during the twenty years of my absence'.

## 44

He said his father was travelling with another fellow through Wales, and, one night, they stopped at a[1] little inn, where there were some other fellows and they joined the other fellows, and spent the evening with them.

They had a very jolly evening,[2] and sat up late,[3] and, by the time they came to go to bed, they (this was when George's father was a very young man) were slightly jolly[4] too. They (George's father and George's father's friend) were to sleep in the same room, but in different beds. They took the candle, and went up. The candle lurched up against the wall[5] when they got into the room, and went out,[6] and they had to undress and grope into bed in the dark. This they did;[7] but, instead of getting into[8] separate beds, as they thought they were doing, they both climbed into the same one without knowing it—one getting in[9] with his head at the top,[10] and the other crawling in[9] from the opposite side of the compass, and lying[9] with his feet on the pillow.

There was silence for a moment,[11] and then George's father said:

'Joe.'

'What's the matter, Tom?' replied Joe's voice from the other end of the bed.

'Why, there's a man[12] in my bed,' said George's father; 'here's his feet on my pillow.'

JEROME K. JEROME

[1] *R.S.* 464.

[2] It is more idiomatic to say 'spent the evening in a very jolly manner' (ве́село).

[3] N.B. заси́живаться (засиде́ться) and see Passage 18, note 4.

[4] Here навеселе́ (adverb) or подвы́пившие, which are both colloquial words.

[5] Perhaps свеча́ уда́рилась (сту́кнулась) о́б стену would be best here. Expressive verbs such as накрени́лась (often of a ship), or качну́лась, followed by к would suggest lurching in one direction but not making contact (they would not be followed by о).

[6] Do not confuse га́снуть (пога́снуть), past tense пога́с, пога́сла, and the transitive verb гаси́ть (погаси́ть) 'to put out'.

[7] они́ так и сде́лали.

[8] вме́сто того́, что́бы лечь в . . .

[9] Either use finite verbs, or say оди́н укла́дываясь (ложа́сь) . . . друго́й вполза́я, &c.

[10] в голова́х, a somewhat colloquial equivalent of в изголо́вьи, can translate 'at the top (head) of the bed' as opposed to в нога́х 'at the foot'. But to avoid the combination голово́й в голова́х, it might be better to say голово́й к поду́шке.

[11] Say 'a moment's silence' (мину́тное).

[12] ещё кто-то 'someone else'.

## 45

About ten minutes more passed, and then they found themselves in the centre of the maze. Harris thought at first of pretending that that[1] was what he had been aiming at; but the crowd looked dangerous, and he decided to treat[2] it as an accident.

Now at least they did know where they were, and the map was once more consulted, and the thing seemed simpler than ever, and off they started for the third time.

And about three minutes later[3] they were back in the centre again.

After that they simply couldn't get anywhere else.[4] Whatever way they turned[5] brought them back to the middle. It became so regular at length, that some of the people stopped there, and waited[6] for the others to take a walk round, and come back to them. Harris drew out his map again, after a while, but the sight of it only infuriated the mob, and they told him to go and curl his hair with it.[7] Harris said that he couldn't help feeling that, to a certain extent, he had become unpopular.

They all got crazy at last, and sang out for the keeper, and the man came and climbed up the ladder outside, and shouted out directions to them. But all their heads were, by this time,[8] in such a confused whirl[9] that they were incapable of grasping anything, and so the man told them to stop where they were,[10] and he would come to them. They huddled together, and waited; and he climbed down, and came in.

JEROME K. JEROME

[1] Work in the word и́менно.  [2] изобрази́ть де́ло.

[3] *R.S.* 538.  [4] Say 'get away from there'.

[5] Use бы and the imperfective aspect (because of the repeated action). Either свора́чивать or повора́чивать is possible.

[6] *R.S.* 390 (i).

[7] Say 'to use it for curling papers'. In this context пусти́ть (followed

by на) may be used idiomatically to translate 'use'. *R.S.* 654 (ii). Cf. the similar usage with a different preposition пусти́ть по́ле под рожь 'to turn a field over to rye'. *R.S.* 654 (iv). [8] *R.S.* 549.
[9] Say 'in their heads there was such confusion'.
[10] постоя́ть на ме́сте. *R.S.* 231.

## 46

At[1] his first, very short, interrogation which took place in his cell immediately after his arrest, he repeated what he had said during[2] the search; he had picked up the leaflets in the street where they were lying, done up in a bundle, and had put them in the book in which they had been discovered. Had he read them? Yes. Why had he not destroyed them? He had meant to destroy them when the fire was[3] lit, but it was summer and he had felt no urgency, since he had not attached great importance to them. But had he not realized that the person[4] of his Majesty the Emperor was maligned in them? Yes, he had realized that, but he had thought that they were old leaflets, of a kind which, according to report, had been common[5] in 1905, and that someone had lost them. That was all. The interrogation was conducted by an officer of the secret police who, when he entered, introduced himself as Lt.-Colonel Polotentsev, said that the investigation of the affair would be in his hands,[6] and added that if Kirill had any complaints, he could address them to[7] the assistant public prosecutor—indicating with a glance his companion who maintained a forbidding silence.[8] After the interrogation he announced that Kirill would be allowed[9] a bath and a parcel of linen, and that if he wished to read he could have a copy of the Gospels.

*Translated and adapted from* KONSTANTIN FEDIN

[1] *R.S.* 558 (i). [2] *R.S.* 539 (i). [3] Tense?
[4] Cf. неприкоснове́нность ли́чности 'sanctity of the person'.

[5] The meaning here is that they had been common habitually throughout the year. Translate 'had been' accordingly using an impersonal construction, 'of which, according to report, there had been many'.

[6] Use an active construction; cf. произвести́ сле́дствие 'to conduct an inquiry'. The emphasis here is on the progress of the action, not its completion and result.

[7] адресова́ть на и́мя.

[8] Say 'was forbiddingly (недосту́пно) silent'.

[9] Place Kirill in the dative case and follow with a past participle passive.

## 47

During his homeward[1] journey, Dibich learned that all the White forces in the South had recognized General Denikin as their Commander-in-Chief, and that Siberia was under the control of Admiral Kolchak, who had proclaimed himself[2] the supreme ruler of Russia. These huge forces in the South and East, comprising all the Cossacks[3] and almost all the officers of the former Russian army, intended to join up along the line of the Volga and close a ring round Moscow which, defending the cause of the Soviets, was unceasingly mobilizing recruits for the Red Army. Dibich had never before heard either of Denikin or Kolchak. But neither[4] had he heard before the Revolution a single one of the names which it had inscribed on the Red banners. He was ashamed of his ignorance and concealed it, explaining it to himself by his lack of education[5] and the fact that he had got out of touch[6] in captivity. It was news to him that there was civil war in the West and North of Russia, as well as in the South and East, that more White armies were in action there under the command of generals of whom he had never heard, and that everywhere the White armies were being opposed by[7] the Soviet army of workers, sailors, and ex-soldiers.

*Translated and adapted from* KONSTANTIN FEDI

[1] Dibich is returning to his native land. *R.S.* 559.

[2] Use a participle.

[3] каза́чество.

4 Say 'But he had not heard also'. 5 неразви́тость.
6 одича́ть. 7 Say 'against the White armies was fighting'.

## 48

I went down to the Marie Céleste that evening,[1] and looked over my cabin, which was extremely comfortable, considering the small size of the vessel. Mr. Goring, whom I had seen in the morning, was to have[2] the one next to mine. Opposite was the captain's cabin and a small berth for Mr. John Harton, a gentleman who was going out in the interests of his firm. These little rooms were arranged on each side of the passage which led from the main-deck to the saloon. The latter[3] was a comfortable room, the panelling[4] tastefully done in oak and mahogany, with a rich Brussels carpet and luxurious settees. I was very much pleased with the accommodation, and also with Tibbs the captain, a bluff, sailor-like fellow with a loud voice, who welcomed me to the ship with effusion, and insisted upon our splitting[5] a bottle of wine in his cabin. He told me that he intended to take his wife and youngest child with him on the voyage,[6] and that he hoped with good luck to make Lisbon in three weeks. We had a pleasant chat and parted the best of friends, he warning[7] me to make the last of my preparations next morning, as he intended to make a start by[8] the mid-day tide, having now shipped all his cargo. I went back to my hotel, where I found a letter from my wife awaiting me, and, after a refreshing night's sleep, returned to the boat in the morning. From this point I am able to quote from the journal which I kept in order to vary[9] the monotony of the long sea-voyage. If[10] it is somewhat bald in places I can at least rely upon its accuracy in details, as it was written conscientiously from day to day.[11]

A. CONAN DOYLE

1 э́тот же ве́чер: э́тот because English 'that' refers to the evening of which the author is speaking.

[2] Use the verb предназнача́ться (предназна́читься).
[3] *R.S.* 456.
[4] 'To panel' in Russian is обшива́ть (обши́ть) пане́лями.
[5] распи́ть.
[6] в рейс. This word can be used of any kind of journey, by air, sea, or land.
[7] The verb предупрежда́ть (предупреди́ть) cannot be followed by an infinitive.
[8] Say 'with'.
[9] скра́шивать (скра́сить) is a good word here. Cf. скра́сить жизнь 'to brighten up one's life'.
[10] A good way to introduce such concessive clauses in Russian is with пусть: cf. пусть по́здно, но я пойду́ 'late though it is, I shall still go'.
[11] *R.S.* 553 (iii).

## 49

About half-past eight Tibbs rushed into my cabin with a very white face and asked me if I had seen[1] his wife. I answered that I had not. He then ran wildly into the saloon. I followed him, endeavouring to persuade[2] him that his fears were ridiculous. We hunted over the ship for an hour and a half without coming on any sign of[3] the missing woman and child. Poor Tibbs lost his voice[4] completely from[5] calling[5] her name. Even the sailors, who are generally stolid[6] enough, were deeply affected by the sight of him as he roamed bareheaded and dishevelled about the deck, searching with feverish anxiety the most impossible places, and returning to them again and again with a piteous[7] pertinacity. The last time she was seen was about seven o'clock, when she took Doddy on to the poop to give him a breath[8] of fresh air before[9] putting him to bed. There was no one there at the time except the black seaman[10] at the wheel, who denies having seen her at all. The whole affair is wrapped in mystery.[11] My own theory is that while Mrs. Tibbs was holding the child and standing near the bulwarks it gave a spring and fell overboard, and that in her attempt to catch or save it, she followed it. I cannot account for the double disappearance in any other way.[12]

It is quite feasible that such a tragedy should be enacted without the knowledge of the man at the wheel, since it was dark at the time, and the peaked skylights[13] of the saloon screen the greater part of the quarterdeck. Whatever the truth may be it is a terrible catastrophe, and has cast the darkest gloom upon our voyage. The mate has put the ship about[14] but there is not the slightest hope of picking them up.

A. CONAN DOYLE

[1] не ви́дел ли я.

[2] *R.S.* 226. Express English 'endeavouring to' by the use of the imperfective aspect in Russian, i.e. убежда́я, possibly strengthening the verb by some adverb such as тще́тно 'vainly'.

[3] но так и не нашли́. Cf. Passage 42, note 5.

[4] Say 'became completely hoarse'.

[5] Use a present gerund. The simple verb крича́ть is intransitive. The appropriate transitive verb is выкри́кивать (вы́крикнуть).

[6] невозмути́мый.

[7] жа́лкий means 'pitiful' or 'wretched', жа́лкое зре́лище 'a pitiful sight'. Say here 'which excited pity', using a participial construction.

[8] Say 'to have a breath of' *R.S.* 231. The Russian verb of motion ('took') may be followed by an infinitive although the subjects are not the same.

[9] *R.S.* 387.

[10] Say 'the sailor negro', cf. Passage 35, note 10.

[11] зага́дочный.

[12] ника́к ина́че.

[13] остроконе́чная застеклённая кры́ша.

[14] положи́л кора́бль на друго́й галс.

## 50

Pyle continued to unpack. He made a little ledge[1] of cases, on which he put his shaving-mirror and tackle. I said: 'I doubt if you'll get any water.'

'Oh,' he said, 'I've enough in the thermos for the morning.'[2] He sat down on his sleeping bag and began to pull off his boots.

'How on earth did you get[3] here?' I asked.

'They let me through as far as[4] Nam Dinh to see[5] our trachoma team,[6] and then I hired a boat.'

'A boat?'

'Oh, some kind of a punt—I don't know the name of it. As a matter of fact, I had to buy it. It didn't cost much!'

'And you came down[7] the river by yourself?'

'It wasn't really difficult, you know. The current was with me.'[8]

'You are crazy.'

'Oh no. The only real danger was[9] running aground.'

'Or being shot up by a naval patrol, or a French plane. Or having your throat cut by the Vietminh.'

He laughed shyly. 'Well, I'm here anyway,' he said.

'Why?'

'Oh, there are two reasons.[10] But I don't want to keep you awake.'

'I'm not sleepy. The guns will be starting soon.'

'Do you mind if[11] I move the candle? It's a bit bright here.' He seemed nervous.

'What's the first reason?'

'Well, the other day you made me think this place was rather interesting.[12] You remember when we were with Granger . . . and Phuong.'

'Yes?'

'I thought I ought to take a look at it.[13] To tell you the truth, I was a bit ashamed of Granger.'

'I see. As simple as all that.'[14]

He began to play with his bootlaces,[15] and there was a long silence. 'I'm not being quite honest,'[16] he said at last.

'No?'

'I really came to see you.'

'You came here to see me?'

'Yes.'

'Why?'

He looked up from his bootlaces in an agony of[17] embarrassment. 'I had to tell you—I've fallen in love with Phuong.'

GRAHAM GREENE

[1] подстáвка or пóлка. [2] *R.S.* 302. [3] *R.S.* 336.
[4] *R.S.* 519 (v). [5] The meaning of 'see' here is 'inspect'.

[6] See Passage 34, note 5. [7] спусти́лись по.
[8] Say 'I was sailing with the current'.
[9] Say 'There was only one danger—I might have run aground'.
[10] *R.S.* 620. [11] мо́жно. [12] Say 'that here it was interesting'.
[13] Say 'to drop in here'.
[14] Say 'and is that all?' то́лько и всего́?.
[15] Use игра́ть followed by the instrumental without с.
[16] Say 'I have not told you the whole truth'. The negation refers to 'whole'—place the negative particle accordingly. In such contexts the accusative and not the genitive is used.
[17] сгора́я (present gerund) от.

## 51

Paul sometimes thought that being poor[1] would not matter if only his father were alive. Then they would still count for something.[2] Instinctively, he knew that they now counted for nothing, and that if they disappeared to-morrow nobody would care. His mother had been sad when his father died, and sometimes she cried when she thought about how poor and helpless they were. But much of the time she seemed to Paul simply to be allowing time to pass over her while she did nothing.[3] She seemed almost not to be able to care;[4] and by not caring,[5] she removed herself from him without even knowing it. Some nights while Paul did his homework she sat at the large table playing patience, concentrating on the game as though it were a great problem. Sometimes after he was asleep[6] she went out alone. She had made[7] several new friends, but she preferred to go to their homes rather than have them come to her,[8] so Paul seldom saw any of them. They all seemed to like dancing and bridge-playing, and he wondered if she went[9] to dances so soon after his father's death. He did not think she did, but he knew she wanted to go. Lately she had begun to talk about their luck changing.[10] Something would turn up and they would again live in a fine house with plenty of clothes and enough of everything.[11] When Paul got older[12] he would have a motor-car of his own and be able to do whatever he pleased. But Paul was old enough[13] already to know that luck had nothing to do with their being alone in three rooms in this side street.

HUGH MACLENNAN

[1] то, что они́ бе́дны.

[2] тогда́ бы с ни́ми счита́лись. Cf. с ним не́чего счита́ться 'he can safely be ignored'.

[3] Say 'It seemed that she, doing nothing, is simply allowing (предоставля́ет) time to pass her by' (скользи́ть ми́мо себя́).

[4] Say 'She, it seemed, was quite incapable of being interested in anything'. [5] Simply всле́дствие э́того. [6] Imperfective.

[7] Use заводи́ть (завести́)... друзе́й, and see Passage 22, note 9.

[8] Use imperfective aspects for all the verbs and invert the order: 'she preferred not to invite them home, but to go to them'.

[9] i.e. 'if she had started going again': *начала́* ли она́ ходи́ть, or alternatively хо́дит ли она́ *уже́*.

[10] i.e. their 'fate' or 'fortune' (судьба́). Say 'talk about the fact that their fate might change'.

[11] всего́ вдо́воль. Cf. too the use of this word as an adverb: вдо́воль нае́сться 'to eat to one's heart's content'.

[12] Use simple futures, подрастёт, &c.

[13] Say 'big enough'.

## 52

For eleven years[1] from the time he left the farm and came to Detroit to live, Henry Ford was never without[2] some sort of horseless carriage[3] in his workshop. All his spare money went to[4] buying parts and spare time to solving problems. He built cars with two cylinders,[5] then with four; he sold them, and they ran,[6] and he saw to it that they continued to run.

Also he tried to establish relations with the business world and with business men; but he never had much success in finding men to share his ideas.[7] The business people wanted to make money out of[8] selling horseless carriages, and as they saw the problem, it was to find some well-to-do person who could[9] afford an expensive toy; they had to find out exactly what kind of toy he wanted, and build it for him and get his money.

But Henry Ford insisted upon looking at the matter from an entirely different angle. The horseless carriage was not[10] a toy for the rich,[11] but a useful article for everybody. It was foolish asking anybody[12] what he wanted because he had no way of knowing what he wanted until he saw it.[13] Go ahead and produce a lot of carriages that could be sold at a low price, and that would run and keep on running. This product would advertise itself[14] on the road, and very soon you would be producing them wholesale,[15] and make a fortune without trying. 'Who will make a fortune with me?' asked Mr. Ford, and could find no volunteers.

He went in with[16] a group of men who called themselves[14] the Detroit Motor Company. He was chief engineer, but he could not control the selling, or the kind of cars produced; so he quickly became dissatisfied, and went back to his own little shop, the one place where he could have his own way.

UPTON SINCLAIR

[1] Say 'All the eleven years'.

[2] Cf. у него́ де́ньги не перево́дятся 'he is never without money' For the omission of 'never' in Russian see Passage 42, note 5. Used positively переводи́ться (перевести́сь) means 'to die out' (of a species).

[3] коля́ска is the best word here since it signifies a four-wheeled sprung vehicle with a raisable top.

[4] Cf. все де́ньги ушли́ на упла́ту долго́в. Use nouns in Russian for the English participles.

[5] Say 'with a two-cylinder engine'. *R.S.* 750 (vi).

[6] они́ дви́гались.

[7] Say 'his searches (по́иски) for . . . were rarely crowned with success'. Note that по́иски is followed by a simple genitive without preposition. Work in the word единомы́шленник.

[8] Cf. на спекуля́циях купе́ц нажи́л миллио́ны. The verb нажива́ть (нажи́ть) used with or without the reflexive pronoun себе́ can also mean 'to acquire something unpleasant through one's way of life', e.g. нажи́ть (себе́) враго́в.

[9] Present tense.

[10] Translate the remainder of this paragraph as if it were reported speech i.e. 'he said that the horseless carriage was not . . .').

[11] Say 'rich men'. *R.S.* 153 (ii).

[12] Here a definite person is envisaged. *R.S.* 514 (iii).

[13] Some re-casting of the English is necessary here. Say, for example:

'show him the thing, then he will know what he should want'. *R.S.* 275.

[14] рекламироваться and называться would mean 'to be advertised', 'to be called'. Use the full form of the reflexive pronoun.

[15] Say 'organize mass production'. налаживать (наладить) is a good verb for 'organize' in this context.

[16] войти в соглашение с.

## 53

I fell into the habit[1] of dropping in to see Isabel three or four times a week in the afternoon after my day's work was over. She was generally[2] alone at that[3] hour and glad to have a gossip.[4] The persons to whom Elliott had introduced her were much older than she, and I discovered that she had few friends of her own generation. Mine were for the most part busy till[5] dinnertime and I found it more agreeable to talk with Isabel than to go to my club and play bridge[6] with rather grouchy Frenchmen who did not particularly welcome the intrusion of a stranger.[7] Her charming way of treating me as if she and I were of an age made conversation easy[8] and we joked and laughed and chaffed one another, chatting now about ourselves, now about our common acquaintances, now about books and pictures,[9] so that the time passed very agreeably. One of the defects of my character is that I can never grow used to the plainness of people;[10] however sweet a disposition a friend of mine may have, years of intimacy can never reconcile me to his bad teeth or lopsided nose; on the other hand I never cease to delight in his comeliness and after twenty years of familiarity I am still able to take pleasure in[11] a well-shaped brow or the delicate line of a cheekbone. So I never came into Isabel's presence without[12] feeling anew a little thrill of pleasure[13] in the perfection of her oval face, in the creamy delicacy of her skin and in the bright warmth of her hazel eyes.

W. SOMERSET MAUGHAM

[1] Use the expression завести́ (приобрести́) привы́чку.

[2] *R.S.* 326 (iii).

[3] Translate в э́то вре́мя. The meaning of э́то here is the time of which the author is speaking.

[4] *R.S.* 231.

[5] The meaning here is 'right up to'. See a similar expression of place in Passage 5, note 4.

[6] Say 'to play bridge in my club'.

[7] Work in непро́шенных партнёров.

[8] Say 'She had a charming way . . . and, thanks to this . . .'. There are two nouns in Russian which mean a person of the same age, све́рстник and рове́сник. In Russian it would probably be best to divide this sentence with a semi-colon at 'easy'.

[9] Say 'painting'. [10] Say 'to people with plain faces'.

[11] получа́ть удово́льствие при ви́де.

[12] Say 'at every meeting with Isabel I felt anew'.

[13] прия́тный тре́пет, гля́дя на.

## 54

Having noted these facts, the detective walked over to the body and knelt down beside it. Taking a magnifying glass from his pocket, he closely examined the back of the head, but beyond a slight discolouration of the flesh[1] under the hair at the base[2] of the skull there was no sign of a wound—nothing to indicate the nature of the weapon with which the blow had been dealt. The body, as has been said, was lying face downwards, with the head resting[3] on one crooked arm, whilst the other arm was stretched out at the side. The legs pointed practically to the wall between[4] the two French windows, the head being just past[5] the corner of the writing-table. The face was practically invisible, buried as it was[6] in the coat sleeve, so the detective left it for the moment, turning his attention to the hands and soles of the feet. The latter appeared to interest him, for he scrutinized them closely through his magnifying glass and rubbed his finger gently on the sole of one. He next turned his attention to the carpet round the body and near the windows, picking up some small pieces of grit[7] which he found on it and placing them carefully in an envelope. Having done this, he rose to his feet and stretched himself.

'Suppose I'd better let them have this body now,' he said. 'Otherwise they'll be worrying me for it,[8] and I want a couple of hours to myself.'

He moved to the door, unlocked it, and put his head outside.

'Jones!' he called. 'Ah, there you are.[9] Bring your things along now, but mind you don't touch anything—anything, mind.[10] Has that ambulance come yet?'

'Yes, sir; it's been here ten minutes.'

'Right. Just tell the chap we shan't keep him much longer.'

HENRY WADE

[1] подтёк на ко́же. [2] ни́жняя часть.

[3] Use уби́тый for 'the body' and continue опира́ясь голово́й на (followed by the accusative).

[4] There is a single Russian word for the wall space between doors or windows—просте́нок.

[5] приходи́лась как раз по ту сто́рону. The verb приходи́ться (прийти́сь) is useful to express location, often expressed in English by 'fall'; cf. ударе́ние прихо́дится на пе́рвом сло́ге 'the stress falls on the first syllable'.

[6] уткну́тое (в + acc.). Omit 'as it was' and say 'since it was buried . . .'. [7] песчи́нки (cf. песчи́нка в глаз попа́ла).

[8] Omit. [9] вот и ты. [10] ничего́, понима́ешь.

## 55

I had known the Phat Diem well in the days before the attack—the one long narrow street of wooden stalls,[1] cut up every[2] hundred yards by a canal, a church and a bridge.[3] At night it had been lit only by candles or small oil lamps (there was no electricity in Phat Diem except in the French officers' quarters), and day or night the street was packed[4] and noisy. In its strange medieval way,[5] it had been[6] the most living town in all the country, and now when I landed and walked up to the officers' quarters it was the most dead. Rubble and broken glass and the smell of burnt paint and plaster, the long street empty as far as the sight could reach,[7] it reminded me of a London thoroughfare in the early morning after an all-clear;[8] one expected to see[9] a placard, 'Unexploded Bomb'.

The front wall of the officers' house had been blown out,[10] and the houses across the street were in ruins. Coming down the river from Nam Dinh I had learnt from Lieutenant Peraud what had happened. He was a serious young man, a Freemason, and to him it was like a judgement on[11] the superstitions of his fellows. The Bishop of Phat Diem had once visited[12] Europe and acquired there a devotion to Our Lady of[13] Fatima. When he came home, he built a grotto in her honour in the Cathedral precincts, and he celebrated her feast every year with a procession.[14] Relations with the colonel in charge of the French and Vietnamese troops had always been strained since the day when the authorities had disbanded the Bishop's private[15] army.

GRAHAM GREENE

[1] Use the verb застра́ивать (застро́ить) meaning 'to occupy with buildings'; cf. застро́ить но́выми дома́ми свобо́дный уча́сток земли́ 'to build new houses on an empty patch of land'.

[2] *R.S.* 538.

[3] Say 'every hundred yards on it either stood a church or cut it up a canal or a bridge'. [4] лю́дная.

[5] Say 'This strange medieval town'.

[6] For the expression in Russian of the English pluperfect see *R.S.* 213. Here the verb should be strengthened by some adverb such as ра́ньше. [7] наско́лько хвата́л глаз.

[8] отбо́й возду́шной трево́ги.

[9] Translate 'at any moment it seemed you would see'. Use того́ и гляди́. [10] бо́мбой снесло́. *R.S.* 253. [11] ка́ра за.

[12] In this sense of visiting different places in a country or continent, the best Russian word is побыва́ть; cf. он побыва́л всю́ду 'he's been everywhere'. [13] Use an adjective.

[14] The Russian word for a religious procession is кре́стный ход, meaning 'a procession with crosses, banners, and icons'.

[15] Say 'hired'.

## 56

One does not linger in the neighbourhood of Reading. The town itself is a famous old[1] place, dating from[2] the dim days of King Ethelred, when the Danes anchored[3] their warships in the Kennet, and started from Reading to ravage all the land of Wessex; and here Ethelred and his brother Alfred fought and defeated them, Ethelred doing[4] the praying and Alfred the fighting.

In later years,[5] Reading seems to have been regarded as a handy place to run down to, when matters were becoming unpleasant in London. Parliament generally rushed off to Reading whenever there was a plague on[6] at Westminster; and, in 1625, the Law[7] followed suit, and all the courts were held at Reading. It must have been worth while having a mere ordinary plague now and then in London[8] to get rid of both the lawyers and the Parliament.

During the Parliamentary struggle,[9] Reading was besieged by the Earl of Essex,[10] and a quarter of a century later the Prince of Orange[10] routed King James's troops there.

Henry I lies buried at Reading, in the Benedictine abbey founded by him there, the ruins of which may still be seen; and in this same abbey great John of Gaunt[10] was married to the Lady Blanche.[10]

At Reading lock we came up with a steam launch, belonging to some friends of mine,[11] and they towed us almost as far as[12] Streatley. It is very delightful being towed by[13] a launch. I prefer it myself to rowing. The run would have been more delightful still, if it had not been for[14] a lot of wretched small boats[15] that were continually getting in the way of our launch.

JEROME K. JEROME

[1] *R.S.* 164.

[2] Say 'founded in'. For the case following the preposition, see *R.S.* 533 (ii).

[3] ста́вили.

[4] Such weak participial constructions in English are usually rendered in Russian through the use of the conjunction причём, followed by a verb in the appropriate tense. [5] See note 2 above.

[6] Use the verb вспы́хивать (вспы́хнуть).

[7] The word юсти́ция can mean either 'justice' in the sense of 'legal procedure' (судопроизво́дство) or (as here) 'the national system of juridical institutions'.

[8] 'It must have been worth while for Londoners to suffer . . .' .

[9] Say 'the struggle of Parliament with the King'.

[10] Earl of Essex граф Э́ссекс (both parts declinable).
Prince of Orange принц Ора́нский (both parts declinable).
John of Gaunt Джон Гонт (both parts declinable).
Lady Blanche ле́ди Бланш (neither part declinable).

[11] This means 'certain friends of mine'. *R.S.* 464.

[12] See Passage 50, note 4.

[13] 'To be towed by' идти́ на букси́ре за. [14] *R.S.* 408.

[15] Use the pejorative suffix -онка (лодчо́нки).

# 57

We stopped under the willows by Kempton Park, and lunched. It is a pretty little spot there; a pleasant grass plateau, running along by[1] the water's edge, and overhung[2] by willows. We had just commenced the third course—the bread and jam[3]—when[4] a gentleman in shirt sleeves[5] and a short pipe came along, and wanted to know if we knew that we were trespassing.[6] We said we hadn't given the matter sufficient consideration as yet to enable us to arrive at a definite conclusion on that point, but that, if he assured[7] us on his word as a gentleman that we *were* trespassing, we would, without further hesitation, believe it.

He gave us the required assurance, and we thanked him, but he still hung about, and seemed to be dissatisfied, so[8] we asked him if there was anything further that we could do for him;[9] and Harris, who is of a chummy disposition, offered him a bit of bread and jam.

I fancy he must have belonged to[10] some society sworn to abstain from bread and jam; for he declined it quite gruffly, as if he were vexed at being tempted with it, and he added that it was his duty to turn us off.

Harris said that if it was a duty it ought to be done, and asked the man what was his idea with regard to the best means for accomplishing it.

JEROME K. JEROME

[1] Use тяну́ться, and say 'along the water's edge runs . . .'.

[2] осенённый. Notice another meaning of the verb осени́ть: его́ осени́ло 'it dawned on him'.

[3] *R.S.* 24.

[4] *R.S.* 383 (ii).

[5] Say 'without a jacket'.

[6] 'To trespass' вторга́ться (вторгну́ться) в чужи́е владе́ния.

[7] Tense? Use the verb руча́ться (поручи́ться) and follow with 'on the word of honour (instr. case) of a gentleman'. Notice the use of the same verb in до́ктор не руча́лся за исхо́д опера́ции 'the doctor would not vouch for the success of the operation'.

[8] так что.

[9] Cf. 'What can I do for you?' чем я могу́ вам служи́ть.

[10] *R.S.* 10.

## 58

He understood why French prisoners[1] in Koenigstein had attacked the Russians, accusing them of treachery: Russia's allies had long since ceased to be her allies and he learned that the French, the English, the Japanese, and the Americans had interfered in Russia's affairs in every region where the struggle was raging, in the North and South, in the East and West. He felt uncomfortable because he could make so little sense of[2] what was going on but he saw that many people to whom[3] he listened in stations and in railway carriages understood no more than he, although they had been witnesses of events and even willing or unwilling participants in them while he had been[4] a prisoner. He felt that events would compel him to take someone's side in the struggle but he was strangely unwilling to do so. He was only aware that if he said[5] the Whites were right, then this would mean[5] that the French who were helping them were right and this he positively refused to admit, because, if that were so,[6] the Frenchmen who had attacked him in Koenigstein must be[7] right; and them he had come to hate[8] because[9] they had spoken with hatred of Russia.

*Translated and adapted from* KONSTANTIN FEDIN

[1] Say 'captive Frenchmen'.
[2] Say 'understood so badly', using the verb разбира́ться (разобра́ться) в.
[3] мно́гие, кого́.
[4] *R.S.* 328 (iii). Say 'had been in captivity'.
[5] Future tense. Use 'означа́ть' for 'mean'.
[6] тогда́ вы́шло бы, что.
[7] Say 'were right'.
[8] возненави́дел.
[9] за то, что.

## 59

There were[1] no droshkies in that[2] part of the town either. Ivan Ilych crossed the Neva once more and plunged into[3] the crooked little streets on the Petersburg side. Meditating, talking to himself aloud, he at last lost his way, and wandered about at random through the dusky, deserted streets, till he came out on the embankment of one of the canals. 'What a walk!'[4] he exclaimed[5] with a laugh, as he stopped to take breath and look at his watch. It was exactly five o'clock. A big, open motorcar, showing no headlights,[6] dashed round[7] the corner, the snow crunching beneath its tyres.[8] At the wheel was an officer in an unbuttoned overcoat; his narrow, cleanshaven face was pale, and his eyes glassy,[9] like those of an extremely drunk man. Behind him sat another officer, his cap pushed well back;[10] his face was not visible and he was holding in both hands a long bundle wrapped in matting.[11] The third person in the car was a civilian, in a tall sealskin cap, with his coat collar turned up. He suddenly rose and gripped the shoulder of the man at the wheel. The car drew up not far from the little bridge. Ivan Ilych watched all three[12] of them jump out, drag the bundle from the car, trail it[13] a few paces over the snow, and then, with an effort, lift it and carry it to the middle of the bridge, heave it over[14] the parapet, and cast it into the water. The officers immediately returned to the car; the civilian,[15] bending over the railing, looked down for a while and then, turning his collar down, ran after his comrades at a rapid trot. The car started off with a jerk[16] and disappeared.

*Translated and adapted from* A. TOLSTOY

[1] This sentence should be re-cast in Russian to read 'Droshkies and in that part of the town there did not turn out to be'. *R.S.* 52 (ii).
[2] э́тот meaning the part of which the author is speaking.
[3] углуби́лся в.
[4] ну и прогу́лочка.
[5] Do not translate 'he exclaimed'. Follow прогу́лочка with a dash, then say 'Ivan Ilych, taking breath, stopped, gave a laugh, and looked at his watch'.
[6] Say 'with headlights extinguished'.
[7] *R.S.* 611. The meaning is 'round the corner towards the person in question' and the correct preposition is из-за. Cf. уе́хать за грани́цу, верну́ться из-за грани́цы 'to go (return from) abroad'.
[8] Say simply 'crunching (скрипя́) the snow'. Cf. звя́кать ключа́ми 'to jingle one's keys'. Omit 'beneath its tyres' which is not in the original Russian.
[9] Use the past participle active of остекляне́ть (perfective) meaning 'to become glazed'.
[10] Cf. from the same author ша́пка с'е́хала ему́ на у́хо, 'his hat had slid down over his ear'. Say 'in a cap which had slid down on to the back of his head'.
[11] The original is дли́нный рого́жный свёрток.
[12] *R.S.* 752.
[13] проволокли́.
[14] перевали́ли че́рез.
[15] Insert же.
[16] рвану́л (the reflexive form is also used with this meaning).

## 60

Somehow it seemed as though the farm had grown richer without making the animals themselves any richer[1]—except, of course, for the pigs and the dogs. Perhaps this was partly because[2] there were so many pigs and so many dogs.

It was not that[3] these creatures did not work, after their fashion.[4] There was, as Squealer[5] was never tired of explaining, endless work in the supervision[6] and organization of the farm. Much of this work was of a kind that the other animals were too ignorant to understand.[7] For example, Squealer told them that the pigs had to expend enormous labours every day upon mysterious things called 'files', 'reports', 'minutes', and 'memoranda'. These were large sheets of paper[8] which had to be closely covered with writing,[9] and as soon as they were so covered, they were burnt in the furnace. This was of the highest importance for the welfare of the farm, Squealer said. But still, neither pigs nor dogs produced any food by their own labour; and there were very many of them, and their appetites were always good.

As for the others, their life, so far as they knew, was as it had always been. They were generally hungry, they slept on straw, they drank from the pool, they laboured in the fields; in winter they were troubled by[10] the cold, and in summer by the flies. Sometimes the older ones among them[11] racked their dim memories[12] and tried to determine whether in the early days of the Rebellion, when Jones's expulsion was still recent, things had been better or worse than now. They could not remember.

GEORGE ORWELL

[1] Use разбогате́ть again, and say 'without the animals having grown richer'.

[2] отча́сти причи́ной э́тому . . . бы́ло то, что. *R.S.* 44 (ii).

[3] не то, что́бы. *R.S.* 394 (iv).

[4] на свой лад.

[5] Some suggestions are фиска́л, я́бедник, i.e. a 'squealer' in the sense of 'a sneak', 'tell-tale', or 'informer'; and more onomatopœically писку́н.

[6] Say 'the supervision . . . required endless work'.

[7] Say 'through (по + dat.) their ignorance did not understand'. 'To understand' in this context may be well rendered by разбира́ться (разобра́ться) в + prep.

[8] *R.S.* 17.

[9] Use испи́сывать (исписа́ть), and see *R.S.* 244 for other examples of the из- prefix with the meaning of 'covering whole surfaces'.

[10] донима́ть (доня́ть) is a good word here. Use the active voice.

[11] те из них, что (кто, кото́рые) бы́ли поста́рше. Что is the most colloquial of the three relative pronouns.

[12] Some possible renderings are напряга́ли свою́ потускне́вшую па́мять, or ры́лись в свое́й потускне́вшей (ту́склой) па́мяти.

# 61

The incident I have just described was not without its aftermath.[1] Like many people who are self-controlled and sure of themselves,[2] Anne would not make concessions; and when, on the terrace, she had let me go, she was acting against her principles. She had of course guessed something, and it would have been easy enough for her[3] to make me talk, but at the last moment she had given in to pity or[4] indifference. It was just as hard for her to make allowances for my shortcomings, as to try to improve[5] them, in both cases she was merely prompted by a sense of duty; in marrying my father she felt she must also take charge of me. I would have found it easier to accept[6] her constant disapproval if she had sometimes shown exasperation,[7] or any other feeling which went more than skin deep. One gets used to other people's[8] faults if one does not feel it a duty to correct them. Within a few months she would have ceased to trouble about me and her indifference might then have been tempered by affection. This attitude would just have suited[9] me. But it could never happen with her, because her sense of responsibility was too strong.

FRANÇOISE SAGAN (*translated Irene Ash*)

[1] не прошёл (or не оста́лся) без после́дствий.

[2] Say 'are characterized by self-control and self-confidence'.

[3] Say 'without difficulty could have'.

[4] This is a good opportunity to use the construction не то . . . не то: translate the verb by поддала́сь.

[5] Say 'correct'. In this sense of moral correction use исправля́ть (испра́вить); cf. исправи́тельный дом 'reformatory'. This verb is also

used of correcting a text; cf. изда́ние второ́е, испра́вленное и допо́лненное. [6] Cf. Passage 92, note 5.

[7] выходи́ла из терпе́ния: continue 'or at least shown some deep feeling . . .'. [8] Remember the adjective чужо́й.

[9] устра́ивать (устро́ить) is a good verb here.

## 62

'Ugliness is one of the seven deadly[1] virtues, Gladys. You, as a good Tory, must not underrate them. Beer, the Bible, and the seven deadly virtues have made our England what she is.'[2]

'You don't like your country, then?' she asked.

'I live in it.'

'That you may censure it the better.'

'Would you have me take the verdict of Europe on it?'[3] he inquired.

'What do they say of us?'

'That Tartuffe has emigrated to England and opened a shop.'

'Is that yours, Harry?'

'I give it to you.'[4]

'I could not use it. It is too true.'

'You need not be afraid. Our countrymen never recognize a description.'[5]

'They are practical.'

'They are more[6] cunning than practical. When they make up their ledger, they balance[7] stupidity by wealth, and vice by hypocrisy.'

'Still, we have done great things.'

'Great things have been thrust on us,[8] Gladys.'

'We have carried their burden.'

'Only as far as the Stock Exchange.'

She shook her head.

'I believe in the race,' she cried.

'It represents the survival of the pushing.'[9]

'It has development.'

'Decay fascinates me more.'

'What of Art?'[10] she asked.

'It is a malady.'

'Love?'

'An illusion.'

'Religion?'

'The fashionable substitute for Belief.'

'You are a sceptic?'

'Never! Scepticism is the beginning of Faith.'

'What are you?'

'To define is to limit.'

'Give me a clue.'[11]

'Threads[11] snap. You would lose your way in the labyrinth.'

'You bewilder me. Let us talk of something else.'

OSCAR WILDE

[1] сме́ртный, not смерте́льный' is used with грех to translate 'deadly sin'. In general, смерте́льный corresponds to English 'fatal', 'deadly'; сме́ртный to 'death' — ('death penalty', 'death bed', 'death sentence', &c.). Both may be translated into English by 'mortal'.

[2] тем, что она́ есть.

[3] Say 'agree with the verdict', and omit 'on it'.

[4] Perhaps уступа́ю его́ вам.

[5] In a general statement like this, put the noun in the plural.

[6] 'more' = 'rather' скоре́е.

[7] If one uses своди́ть (свести́) бала́нс to translate 'make up the ledger', 'to balance' may well be rendered by погаша́ть (погаси́ть), which is commonly used in this meaning of cancelling out one thing by another. The simple imperfective, гаси́ть, may also have this meaning of 'to cancel', 'pay off', or 'render invalid'.

[8] Use the active voice. A simple dative is required after навя́зывать (навяза́ть). N.B. Do not confuse the three verbs (i) навя́зывать (навяза́ть) 'to tie on', 'impose', 'foist'; (2) навяза́ть (навя́знуть) 'to stick'; (3) навяза́ть, perfective verb, 'to tie, bind, or knit *a lot* of something'.

[9] выжива́ние наибо́лее предприи́мчивых.

[10] ну, а иску́сство?

[11] The same Russian word нить can translate both nouns. 'A' in the sense of 'just one' ('give me just one clue', 'give me a clue at least') can be rendered idiomatically by хоть.

## 63

Husein awoke because his body rolled over on the bunk and his head struck[1] the steel wall of the cabin. He at once felt a chill, and turning his head towards the porthole,[2] he opened his eyes. Through the round opening filtered dim, grey light in which danced[3] fine drops of spray. Husein remembered that the previous night, before he went to sleep,[4] he had been lying in the same position, looking through the porthole, and in[5] the velvety, dark blue sky, he had seen, as if through a telescope, a large light blue star. Now the air outside[6] was filled with a hollow[7] rumble as though someone with an enormous soft fist were regularly pounding[8] the side of the ship. There was a ceaseless murmur of water[9], trickling from somewhere[10] above.

Husein jumped down on to the floor, swayed, and caught hold of[11] the edge of the bunk. He stood still for a short while,[12] stretching himself and spreading out his arms in case of accidents.[13] Voices and foot-steps were audible from the other side of the wall and he stood motionless,[14] listening, his jersey over his head.[15] Finally he pulled it on, put on his jacket, and pulled his cap well down[16] so that the wind would not blow it off.[17]

In the passage he ran into Dogailo, warming his back against the wall of the galley. The bosun's oilskins were black[18] with water and strands of wet, grey hair were clinging[18] to his forehead. He looked slightly shamefaced, as if he had been caught doing something wrong.

*Translated and adapted from* YURI KRYMOV

[1] A preposition is necessary after 'struck' in Russian. *R.S.* 636.
[2] иллюминáтор.
[3] кружи́лись.
[4] Use a preposition and noun construction. *R.S.* 548.
[5] *R.S.* 561.
[6] Say 'outside, everything'.
[7] глухóй. This is a useful word, with a number of different equivalents in English: глухáя жéнщина 'a deaf woman', глухóе недовóльство 'vague dissatisfaction', глухáя дереву́шка 'a remote hamlet', глухóй соглáсный 'an unvoiced consonant', гдухáя стенá 'a blank wall'.

[8] Insert a preposition in Russian. Cf. в о́кна бил дождь.

[9] Say 'Ceaselessly murmured water trickling . . .'.

[10] From some definite though unknown place. *R.S.* 483.

[11] ухвати́лся за. Note also the figurative use of this verb: все с ра́достью ухвати́лись за э́ту мысль 'everyone grasped eagerly at this idea'.

[12] *R.S.* 231.

[13] на вся́кий слу́чай. The commonest meaning of this expression is 'in case of need', or 'just in case'.

[14] засты́л на ме́сте. Застыва́ть (засты́ть) is a useful verb. Я засты́л от стра́ха 'I was petrified with fear', солда́ты вы́тянулись и засты́ли 'the soldiers stood erect and froze to the spot', засты́вшая улы́бка 'a frozen smile'.

[15] накры́тый с голово́й фуфа́йкой.

[16] надви́нул поглу́бже.

[17] *R.S.* 253.

[18] Use perfective verbs with resultative meanings 'had become black', 'had clung to'.

## 64

Like many old sailors, Evgeni Stepanovich Kutasov was superstitious. In spring, setting out to fish inshore,[1] he would leave a pinch of tobacco on the beach so as not to lose his tackle. When his boat got into a stretch of still water[2] and the sail drooped[3] like a rag[4] from the mast, Evgeni Stepanovich would whistle[5] quietly through his teeth to call up a wind.

Sometimes a wind would actually spring up and fill out his sail like a bladder.[4] The boat would heel and skim merrily along.[6] Evgeni Stepanovich neither rejoiced nor thought very much about it—the wind was there and that was that.[7] But sometimes the sparkling mirror of still water stretched as far as[8] the horizon, merging with the torrid[9] sky, and no amount of whistling could summon even the slightest breeze. Then Evgeni Stepanovich did not despair but took to the oars.

Solitary outings were Captain Kutasov's favourite pastime. Dropping in for a drink with[10] elderly pilots, he loved to chat with them about his old job. He himself had finished with seafaring long ago and worked in the records department[11] of the Caspian steamship-line.

Sailing inshore on his days off, he would gaze after[12] the ships putting out to[13] sea until their curling, transparent smoke disappeared on the horizon. Then he would cast a glance at the shore, separated from him by a narrow strip of dirty water, and a vague nagging[14] feeling would fill his heart, like a traveller's longing for his native heath. But memories held[15] danger for him, and he was afraid to look into his past.

*Translated and adapted from* YURI KRYMOV

[1] на взмóрье. The noun взмóрье can mean either 'coastal waters' or 'sea-shore'. [2] штиль. [3] обвисáл.

[4] *R.S.* 46 (ii).

[5] The verb used here is посви́стывать, which means 'to whistle quietly and sporadically'. The verb свистéть would describe a louder, more piercing whistle. Used with the dative case свистéть means 'to whistle in disapproval'; cf. ви́жу, что нéкоторые зри́тели со злóбой мне свистя́т. [6] бежáла рéзво. [7] — и лáдно.

[8] *R.S.* 519 (v).

[9] раскалённый; cf. раскалённый песóк 'scorching sand'.

[10] Say 'stopping at the pub' (пивнáя). [11] отдéл учёта.

[12] провожáл глазáми. [13] Say 'going away to'.

[14] Use the present participle active of сосáть. Cf. смýтная, нея́сная тревóга сосáла егó. [15] тáили в себé.

## 65

Soames had travelled little. Aged nineteen he had made the 'petty tour'[1] with his father, mother, and Winifred—Brussels, the Rhine, Switzerland, and home by way of Paris. Aged twenty-seven, just when he began to take interest in pictures,[2] he had spent five hot weeks in Italy, looking into[3] the Renaissance—not so much in it as he had been led to expect[4]—and a fortnight in Paris on his way back, looking into[3] himself, as became[5] a Forsyte surrounded by people so strongly self-centred and 'foreign'[6] as the French. His knowledge of their language being derived from his public school, he did not understand them when they spoke. Silence he had found better for all parties; one did not make a fool of oneself. . . .[7] He was too cautious and too shy to explore that side of Paris supposed by Forsytes to constitute its attraction under the rose;[8] and as for a collector's[9] bargain—not one to be had! As Nicholas might have put it— they were a grasping lot.[10] He had come back uneasy, saying Paris was overrated.

When, therefore, in June of 1900, he went to Paris, it was but his third attempt on[11] the centre of civilization. This time, however, the mountain was going to Mahomet;[12] for he felt by now more deeply civilized than Paris, and perhaps he really was. Moreover, he had a definite objective. This was no mere genuflexion to a shrine[13] of taste and immorality, but the prosecution of his own legitimate affairs. He went, indeed, because things were getting past a joke.[14]

JOHN GALSWORTHY

[1] соверши́л «малый круг».

[2] Not any particular ones. Say 'painting' жи́вопись.

[3] Of the various verbs which may go with both objects, вника́я в + acc. or присма́триваясь к + dat. are perhaps the best.

[4] в кото́ром, одна́ко, он нашёл ме́ньше, чем ожида́л.

[5] как подоба́ет. Note the present tense, and the fact that подоба́ет suggests the slightly dated English perhaps better than надлежи́т or подхо́дит.

[6] чу́ждый. Чужо́й means primarily belonging to someone else, the property or work of someone else.

[7] не стро́ишь из себя́ дурака́.

[8] кото́рая, как предполага́ют Форса́йты, и явля́ется его́ та́йной прима́нкой. Note the word order, tense, and particle и.

[9] The possessive adjective from коллекционе́р is коллекционе́рский.

[10] *R.S.* 103.

[11] покуше́ние на. Cf. the use of покуше́ние to translate' an attempt on a person's life'.

[12] Quite literally: гора́ пришла́ к Маго́мету.

[13] коленопреклоне́ние пе́ред алтарём or стоя́ние на коле́нях пе́ред.

[14] де́ло уже́ перестава́ло быть шу́ткой (принима́ло серьёзный оборо́т).

# 66

Soames was forced, therefore, to set the blame entirely down to[1] his wife. He had never met a woman so capable of inspiring affection. They could not go anywhere without[2] his seeing how all the men were attracted by her; their looks, manners, voices, betrayed it; her behaviour under this attention[3] had been beyond reproach. That she was[4] one of those women—not too common in the Anglo-Saxon race—born to be loved and to love, who when not loving are not living, had certainly never even occurred to him. Her power of attraction[5] he regarded as part of her value as his wife; but it made him, indeed, suspect[6] that she could give as well as receive; and she gave him nothing! 'Then why did she marry me?' was his continual thought. He had forgotten his courtship;[7] that year and a half[8] when he had besieged[9] and lain in wait for her, devising[10] schemes[11] for her entertainment, giving[10] her gifts, proposing[10] to her periodically, and keeping[10] her other admirers away with his perpetual presence. He had forgotten the day when, adroitly taking advantage of her dislike to her home surroundings, he crowned his labours with success. If he remembered anything, it was[12] the dainty capriciousness[13] with which the golden-haired, dark-eyed girl had treated him. He certainly did not remember the look on her face when suddenly one day she had yielded, and said that she would marry him.

JOHN GALSWORTHY

[1] во всём вини́ть.

[2] Say 'Wherever they went together, Soames invariably noticed . . .'. English double negatives are commonly rendered in Russian in this way. Since the emphasis is not on the actual motion, but on being in different places, появля́ться (появи́ться) might well be used here (with где бы ни).

[3] Say 'surrounded by . . . she behaved . . .'.

[4] мысль о том, что . . .

[5] обая́ние.

[6] но э́то наводи́ло на мысль. Наводи́ть (навести́) is a very useful

verb, and commonly governs nouns in combinations where English uses a verb alone, e.g. наводи́ть страх 'frighten'; — ску́ку 'bore'; — поря́док 'tidy up'.

[7] вре́мя своего́ сватовства́.

[8] те полтора́ го́да. *R.S.* 742 (i).

[9] Imperfective aspect.

[10] Use four present gerunds. Notice that подноси́ть (поднести́) is commonly combined with пода́рок. 'To keep away', 'drive away' can be translated by отва́живать (отва́дить).

[11] Say 'all sorts of ways to' вся́ческие спо́собы, что́бы.

[12] Here translate by то то́лько.

[13] капри́зная гра́ция is one possibility.

## 67

And yet the animals never gave up hope. More, they never lost, even for an instant, their sense of honour and privilege in being members[1] of Animal Farm. They were still the only farm in the whole county—in all England!—owned and operated by[2] animals. Not one of them, not even[3] the youngest, not even the newcomers who had been brought from farms ten or twenty miles away,[4] ever ceased to marvel at that. And when they heard the gun booming[5] and saw the green flag fluttering at the masthead, their hearts swelled with[6] imperishable pride, and the talk turned always towards the old heroic days, the expulsion of Jones, the writing of the Seven Commandments, the great battles in which the human[7] invaders had been defeated. None of the old dreams had been abandoned.[8] The Republic of the Animals which Major had foretold, when the green fields of England should be untrodden by[9] human feet, was still believed in. Some day it was coming: it might not be soon, it might not be within the lifetime of any animal now living, but still it was coming. Even the tune of 'Beasts of England' was perhaps hummed secretly here and there: at any rate, it was a fact that[10] every animal on the farm knew it, though no one would have dared to sing it aloud. It might be that their lives were hard and that not all of their hopes had been fulfilled; but they were conscious that they were not as other animals. If they went hungry, it was not from feeding tyrannical human beings;[11] if they worked hard,[12] at least they worked for themselves.

GEORGE ORWELL

[1] Say 'their feeling that belonging to . . . is an honour and a privilege' чу́вство, что принадле́жность к . . . явля́ется че́стью и привиле́гией.

[2] A good literal rendering can be given by saying 'continued to remain the only farm owned' &c., and using present participles in the instrumental case (фе́рмой принадлежа́щей . . . и управля́емой . . . ). Alternatively one may say 'which belonged to . . . and was ruled by them' (управля́лась и́ми).

[3] да́же translates 'not even' as well as 'even'.

[4] Use с with фе́рма in the gen. plural to translate 'from', and either continue (находя́щихся) на расстоя́нии + gen., or simply за + acc. in which case отту́да will translate 'away'. Notice this use of за to denote distance separating one object from another (от), and cf. the syntactical synonym в + prep., followed by от (за де́сять миль от, в десяти́ ми́лях от).

[5] гул is an expressive word to translate the 'booming' of the gun.

[6] Not раздува́лись, which would sound comical in this context, but ши́рились от or some neutral word like переполня́лись + instr.

[7] Perhaps двуно́гий would be most appropriate here.

[8] Say 'They had not renounced (отказа́лись от) a single dream'; and remember that there is no gen. plural of мечта́ (see *R.S.* 74) if it is intended to say 'a single one of their dreams'.

[9] Use the active voice: бо́льше не бу́дет ступа́ть челове́ческая (людска́я) нога́, and notice the idiomatic use of the singular noun.

[10] Avoid факт by some such expression as не подлежи́т сомне́нию, несомне́нно. [11] люде́й-тира́нов (or тира́нов-люде́й).

[12] мно́го, not тяжело́ ! One says тяжёлая рабо́та, but not тяжело́ рабо́тать.

## 68

When Radishchev in his 'Journey from Petersburg to Moscow' wrote the words 'I looked around me and my soul was lacerated by the sufferings of mankind',[1] the Russian Intelligentsia was born. Radishchev was the most remarkable phenomenon in Russia in the eighteenth century. The influence of Rousseau is, of course, to be traced in him, as well as the doctrine of natural law.[2] Radishchev is remarkable not for[3] the originality of his thought but for the originality of his sensitiveness, his aspiration towards truth, righteousness, and freedom. He was grievously wounded by the injustice of serfdom. He was the first to[4] expose[5] it and was one of the first Russian Populists. He stood head and shoulders[6] above those who surrounded him. He asserted the supremacy of conscience. He sympathized very deeply with the French Revolution; but he protests against the lack of freedom of thought and of the press during its height. He preaches self-restraint in the matter of one's own requirements[7] and appeals for the relief of the poor.[8] Radishchev may be regarded as the father[9] of the radical revolutionary tendencies[10] of the Russian Intelligentsia. The main thing for him is not the good of the State but the good of the people. His fate is a premonition of[11] the fate of the revolutionary Intelligentsia; he was condemned to death, but the sentence was commuted to[12] ten years' exile in Siberia.

*Translated and adapted from* N. BERDYAEV

N.B. We have kept the tenses of the original in translating and adapting, in order to show the Russian fondness for changing suddenly from past to present in a historical narrative. See *R.S.* 188 ff.

[1] Radishchev's words were: я взгляну́л окре́ст меня́ — душа́ моя́ страда́ниями челове́чества уязвленна́ ста́ла.

[2] есте́ственное пра́во.

[3] замеча́телен + instr.

[4] он пе́рвый + past tense.

[5] облича́ть (обличи́ть) is a good word here, containing the idea of denunciation as well as exposure. Раскрыва́ть (раскры́ть) and обнару́живать (обнару́жить) rather suggest 'to bring to light', 'bring to the surface', 'discover', or 'reveal something secret'. Обнажа́ть (обнажи́ть) is the nearest equivalent to English 'lay bare'.

[6] Berdyaev says мно́гими голова́ми.

[7] The original reads самоограниче́ние потре́бностей. If one uses самооблада́ние, it will have to be followed by в отноше́нии свои́х потре́бностей.

[8] Use призыва́ет + infinitive.

[9] Here родонача́льник.

[10] тече́ния or направле́ния.

[11] Berdyaev uses the somewhat archaic предваря́ет. Предзнамену́ет

also has an archaic flavour. Modern Russian would probably say предвеща́ет.

[12] смягчён cannot be followed by к (or any other preposition). It must be used absolutely—пригово́р был смягчён—in which case continue и Ради́щев был со́слан. The best and closest translation would be: он был приговорён к сме́ртной ка́зни, но пригово́р э́тот был заменён ссы́лкой . . . (the original has с заме́ной ссы́лкой).

## 69

The religious metaphysics of Leo Tolstoy are less profound and less Christian than the religious metaphysics of Dostoevsky. But Tolstoy was of immense importance to Russian religious thought in the second half of the nineteenth century. Dostoevsky as a religious thinker influenced a comparatively small circle of the intelligentsia; Tolstoy as a religious moral preacher had influence on a wider circle—he exercised a hold over[1] the masses of the people also. His influence was felt in the sectarian movements. Groups of Tolstoyans in the proper sense were not numerous, but the Tolstoyan ethic[2] greatly influenced the moral values[3] of very wide circles of the Russian Intelligentsia. Doubts about the justification[4] for private property, especially land, doubts about the right to judge and to punish, denunciation of the evil and wrong of all forms of state and authority, repentance[5] of one's privileged position, the consciousness of guilt before the working people, a revulsion from[6] war and violence, the dream[7] of the brotherhood of man—all these conditions were peculiar to the average mass of the Russian Intelligentsia. They penetrated too into the highest stratum of Russian society and even took hold of a section of Russian officialdom. The Tolstoyan ethic was considered unrealizable, but yet the most lofty which could be imagined.[8] Such, however, was the attitude towards the Gospel ethics in general.

There was in Tolstoy an extraordinary longing for[9] the perfect life, an acute awareness of his own imperfection.

He derived the awareness of his sinfulness and the inclination towards[10] unceasing repentance from Orthodoxy. The idea that it is first necessary to reform oneself, not to improve the life of other people, is a traditional Orthodox idea.

*Adapted from* N. BERDYAEV

[1] The imperfective захва́тывал used in the original emphasizes the duration of his influence. [2] толсто́вская мора́ль.

[3] Here оце́нки, i.e. evaluations or value-judgements. Cf. це́нности in such phrases as культу́рные, духо́вные це́нности, i.e. things which are valuable.

[4] Berdyaev uses опра́вданность (+ gen., not за).

[5] покая́ние (в + prep.), used mainly in religious contexts, is the word used in the original and approximates to 'confession', 'penitence', and 'penance' in English. Раска́яние is the normal secular word for 'being sorry for one's misdeeds and mistakes'. N.B. the nineteenth-century Russian phenomenon, the раска́явшийся дворяни́н, 'the repentant nobleman'. [6] *R.S.* 692. [7] Not сон!

[8] Notice the idiomatic то́лько in the phrase каку́ю то́лько мо́жно себе́ предста́вить. This intensifying sense is also felt in such combinations as заче́м то́лько? 'why on earth?', кто то́лько? 'who on earth?', and, in the negative, каки́х то́лько книг он не чита́л 'he's read absolutely everything!' [9] жа́жда + gen. (not к).

[10] N.B. the fine distinction in some contexts between скло́нность к 'tendency towards', 'inclination towards' (as here), and накло́нность к 'bent' or 'aptitude for'. Do not confuse with наклоне́ние 'inclination', as the action of the verb 'to incline' or 'bend towards', or, in a grammatical context, 'mood' (cf. склоне́ние 'declension').

## 70

It is true that Dostoevsky's characters are taken almost entirely from the 'Despised and Rejected', as one of his books was[1] called, and often from the ranks[2] of the abnormal: but when a great writer wishes to reveal[3] the greatest adventures[4] and the deepest experiences[5] which the soul of man can undergo,[6] it is vain for him to take the normal type: it has no adventures. The adventures of the soul of

Fortinbras would be of no help[7] to mankind: but the adventures of Hamlet and Don Quixote are a help to mankind and neither are normal types.

Dostoevsky wrote the tragedy of life and of the soul, and to do this he chose circumstances as terrific as those which unhinged the reason of King Lear, shook that of Hamlet and made Oedipus blind himself. His books resemble[8] Greek tragedies by the magnitude of the spiritual adventures they set forth; they are unlike Greek tragedies in the Christian charity[9] and the faith and the hope which goes out of them; they inspire[10] the reader with courage, never with despair, although Dostoevsky, face to face with the last extremities of evil, never seeks to hide it or to shun it, but merely to search for the soul of goodness[11] in it. He did not search in vain, and just as, when he was on his way to Siberia, a conversation he had with a fellow prisoner[12] inspired that man with the feeling that he could go on living and even face penal servitude, so do Dostoevsky's books come to mankind as a message[13] of hope from a radiant country. That is what[14] constitutes his peculiar greatness.

M. BARING

[1] *R.S.* 70.

[2] ряды́: ранг is an *official* rank, category (разря́д), or degree (сте́пень).

[3] Here 'to reveal' means 'to express', 'show', or 'disclose', and therefore пока́зывать (показа́ть) or выска́зывать (вы́сказать) would be appropriate. Открыва́ть (откры́ть) would also get the meaning, but not обнару́живать (обнару́жить) which means primarily 'to discover', 'detect', or 'find out', and not разоблача́ть (разоблачи́ть), 'to expose' or 'unmask' something bad.

[4] приключе́ния rather than похожде́ния which corresponds more to 'escapades'.

[5] i.e. 'things one feels' пережива́ния. О́пыт in the plural means 'experiments', 'essays', in the sense of 'first attempts'. It does not mean 'experiences'.

[6] Use подверга́ться (подве́ргнуться) or испы́тывать (испыта́ть).

[7] The simple future may be used: никако́й по́льзы не принесу́т.

[8] похо́жи на + acc., followed by the simple instrumental.

[9] Here любо́вь. N.B. благотвори́тельность means 'charity' in the sense of 'philanthropy', 'unpaid work'.

[10] Perhaps вселя́ть (всели́ть) что в кого́ is the best word here, where the objects are both 'courage' and 'despair'. Внуша́ть (внуши́ть) что кому́ (чему́) and наполня́ть (напо́лнить) что чем are equally possible, but the verbs возбужда́ть (возбуди́ть) and вдыха́ть (вдохну́ть) are more readily combined with positive or active qualities like 'courage', 'hope', 'life', &c., than with 'despair' (as indeed is the English verb 'inspire'). N.B. вдохновля́ть (вдохнови́ть) is impossible here: this verb means 'inspire' *by* example, or *to* a heroic deed, but not *with* courage.

[11] суть добра́.

[12] това́рищ по ссы́лке.

[13] Say 'are (or 'have become') for the world a message'.

[14] в э́том-то и заключа́ется or э́то-то и составля́ет. Such English constructions as 'that is what', 'this is where', &c., normally go into Russian without circumlocution. See also *R.S.* 448.

# 71

Lady Fanny's sister-in-law, though turned[1] forty now, still retained a youthful bloom in her cheeks, and had no need[2] at all to shrink from the sunlight. Lady Fanny, who had taken care to[3] seat herself with her back to the window, could not help feeling slightly resentful. There really seemed to be little difference between the Duchess and the girl whom Avon had brought to England twenty-four years ago. Leonie's figure was as slim as ever, her hair, worn just now en négligé,[4] was untouched by grey, and her eyes, those great dark-blue eyes which had first attracted the Duke, held all their old sparkle.[5] Twenty-four years of marriage had given her dignity—when she chose[6] to assume it, the feminine wisdom which she had lacked[7] in the old days; but no wifely or motherly responsibility,[8] no weight of honours, of social eminence,[9] had succeeded in subduing the gamin spirit[10] in her. Lady Fanny considered her far too impulsive,[11] but since she was, at the bottom of her somewhat shallow heart, very fond of her sister-in-law, she admitted that Leonie's impetuosity only added to her charm.

GEORGETTE HEYER

[1] ей было за сорок.
[2] *R.S.* 301 and 522.
[3] Use an adverb, нарочно or обдуманно.
[4] причёсанные с нарочитой небрежностью.
[5] искрились попрежнему. This is a useful verb; cf. искрится роса (снег, вода).
[6] ей приходило в голову.
[7] *R.S.* 302.
[8] Say 'despite the duties of wife and mother'.
[9] Say 'the responsibility laid upon (наложенную) her by honours and an eminent position in society'.
[10] Say 'she had preserved her gamin spirit' (мальчишеская бойкость).
[11] импульсивный or порывистый. 'Impetuosity' in the last line may be translated by порывистость or пылкость.

## 72

He caught up with her at Nyon and introduced himself[1]—Benjamin Constant—of all the Constants, the only one Germaine had ever met. His appearance was striking: tall[2] and gangling, in his late twenties;[3] a pale, freckled face surmounted by[4] a shock of flamboyant red hair,[5] braided at the nape and held up by[6] a small comb; a nervous tic; red-rimmed[7] myopic eyes; ironic mouth; a long, finely curved nose; long torso, poor posture,[8] slightly pot-bellied, long-legged—a decidedly gauche, unhandsome, yet interesting and attractive figure of a man, certainly somebody altogether out of the ordinary.[9] Germaine invited him to continue the journey in her carriage. By the time they reached Rolle, Germaine knew that her companion was the most fascinating talker she had ever met. They dined at the house of some of Germaine's friends; at table they had their first argument. Germaine complained against a newspaper which had attacked her father; she was going to have the paper suppressed.[10] Benjamin burst into an impassioned speech[11] in favour of the freedom of the press. Germaine was delighted. They continued their trip to Lausanne, completely absorbed in each other's conversation. When they arrived, Germaine invited him to Mezery, to continue their talk.

Thus began what must have been the most eloquent love affair in history.[12]

J. C. HEROLD

[1] представился (not представил себя).

[2] In this long sentence follow the English as closely as possible; i.e. a series of adjectives and nouns in the nominative: высокий и долговязый блёдное лицо . . ., &c.

[3] лет под тридцать. Cf. 'at the end of the twenties' в конце двадцатых годов. *R.S.* 750 (i).

[4] под копной or над которым возвышалась копна.

[5] A compound adjective such as огненно-рыжий would be appropriate here.

[6] The past participle подхваченный (in the proper case) suggests that it has been caught up; the present participle придерживаемый emphasizes that it continues to be held up.

[7] с красными веками. N.B. 'rim' of spectacles оправа (в роговой оправе 'horn-rimmed').

[8] Translate by an adjective such as нескладный, сутуловатый.

[9] незаурядный is a good word here. 'Figure of a man' cannot be translated literally.

[10] она собиралась добиться запрещения газеты. See *R.S.* 32 (i). 'To suppress a newspaper' запрещать (запретить); —'a rebellion', 'riot', 'yawn' подавлять (подавить); —'the truth' замалчивать (замолчать).

[11] разразился . . . речью. Cf. too this verb with violent actions and emotions: смехом, слезами 'burst out laughing, crying'.

[12] Here роман is better than любовь; continue . . . роман, который знает история.

# 73

Sensibility, passion, enthusiasm, exaltation, happiness, sadness—these words recur constantly in Mme. de Staël's writings, along with[1] love, friendship, kindness, nobility, generosity, virtue: along, also, with reason, light, progress, freedom. All vague words, taken singly,[2] but together they define her spiritual climate and contain all that was sacred to her. When, upon her marriage, she met the world with its mask off,[3] she discovered that the world held all these notions in contempt. The shock lasted a lifetime. Contemptuous laughter at the expense of[4] a generous, idealistic impulse or thought was, to her, the sin against the Holy Ghost. The 'tyranny of ridicule', she explained in *De la littérature*, characterized the final years of the ancien régime in France and was the product of[5] an aristocratic court society in which men were judged according to what they *appeared* to be rather than what they *were*.[6] Every departure from accepted behaviour was its target;[7] 'it laughs at all those who see the earnestness of life[8] and who still believe in true feelings and in serious thought . . . It soils the hope of youth. Only shameless vice is above its reach.'[9] Before the Revolution, this 'discouraging mentality'[10] was, at least, kept in check by a polished taste and the refinement of manners; the Revolution did away with the taste and the manners, leaving only the jeer[11] of those who held money and power to be the one reality, and all the rest a dangerous and contemptible illusion.

J. C. HEROLD

1 наряду́ с. 2 The usual idiom is взя́тые в отде́льности.

3 Perhaps сдёрнувший с себя́ личи́ну (or сорва́вший с себя́ ма́ску) свет.

4 насме́шка над, but смех по по́воду.

5 Say 'was engendered by': была́ порождена́ (if тирани́я is the subject).

6 по тому́, чем они́ каза́лись, а не по тому́, чем они́ бы́ли. The contrast of каза́ться and быть (на са́мом де́ле) is acceptable in this context.

7 мише́нь is commonly associated with ridicule, derision, &c.: ( . . . отклоне́ние) бы́ло для неё мише́нью, or бы́ло мише́нью для её напа́док (taking 'it' to refer to the tyranny of ridicule).

8 Say 'who take a serious attitude to'.

9 неприкоснове́нен для неё.

10 э́тот «обескура́живающий склад ума́» сде́рживался . . .

11 This can be rendered literally: сохрани́в лишь глумле́ние.

## 74

There was a woman who loved her husband, but she could not live with him. The husband, on his side, was sincerely attached to his wife, yet he could not live with her. They were both under forty,[1] both handsome and both attractive. They had the most sincere regard for one another, and felt, in some odd way, eternally married to one another.[2] They knew each other more intimately than they knew anybody else; they felt more known[3] to one another than to any other[4] person.

Yet they could not live together. Usually, they kept a thousand miles apart. But when he sat in the greyness of England, at the back of his mind, with a certain grim fidelity, he was aware of his wife, her strange yearning to be loyal and faithful, having her gallant affairs away in the sun, in the south.[5] And she, as she drank[6] her cocktail on the terrace over the sea, and turned[6] her grey, sardonic eyes on the heavy dark face of her admirer, whom she really liked quite a lot, she was actually preoccupied with[7] the clear-cut[8] features of her handsome young husband,[9] thinking of how he would be asking his secretary to do something for him, asking in that good-natured, confident voice of a man who knows that his request will be only too gladly fulfilled.

The secretary, of course, adored him. She was very competent, quite young, and quite good-looking. She adored him. But then all his servants always did, particularly his women-servants. His men-servants were likely to[10] swindle him.

D. H. LAWRENCE

[1] Say 'had not yet reached the age of forty' (сорокале́тний во́зраст).
[2] Say 'eternally bound by the ties of marriage'.
[3] бли́же и поня́тнее. [4] посторо́нний.
[5] This sentence will have to be re-cast in Russian. Say, for example, 'But with his grim fidelity, even among the mists of England, he

could not for a moment rid himself of a vague awareness that his wife, despite her strange longing for loyalty, was conducting gallant affairs in the far-off sunny south'. 'Rid himself of' отде́латься от.

[6] Use present gerunds 'sipping (отпива́я) . . . looking with grey sardonic eyes'. [7] поглощена́ мы́слями о. [8] точёные.

[9] Place a semi-colon here and continue 'she was imagining'.

[10] Say 'when opportunity offered' (при слу́чае).

# 75

After reading Shchedrin's *The Golovlyov Family*[1] one sees why a character like Iudushka, the liar and humbug, is greater than Pecksniff who is, I suppose, the nearest English parallel. Iudushka is greater, firstly, because he has Russia inside him, and, secondly, because he is encumbered[2] with the dead weight[3] of human dullness[4] and vulgarity.[5] He is greater because he is a bore. I do not mean that Iudushka is boring to read about. I mean that Dickens had no notion that Pecksniff was a boring and vulgar man; Dickens's mind was interested only in the dramatic and absurd exterior of the whited sepulchre.[6] Shchedrin did not stop at the farce of human hypocrisy, for the tricks of hypocrisy are really too crude and blatant.[7] Shchedrin went on collecting the evidence[8] with the patience of one of[9] those static realists like[9] Richardson; and he presently came upon the really terrible thing in Iudushka's character. We can laugh (Shchedrin seems to say) at[10] the obvious hypocrisies of Iudushka and, like his neighbours, we can grin, at his eye-rolling,[11] his genuflexions and his slimy whimsicalities;[12] but there is something more serious. The real evil is the moral stagnation in Iudushka's character. The real evil is the muddle, the tangle of evasions, words, intrigues by which he instinctively seeks to dodge[13] reality. We forgive his sins; what eludes[14] forgiveness is the fact that his nature has gone bad; so that he himself does not know the difference between good and evil.

V. S. PRITCHETT

[1] *R.S.* 13 (iv).
[2] обременён. [3] мёртвый груз. [4] ну́дность.
[5] по́шлость. [6] гроб пова́пленный.
[7] крича́щий or крикли́вый. Крикли́вый may also be used of a voice ('loud, penetrating') or a person ('shrewish, quarrelsome').
[8] Here да́нные 'data, facts'. This word may also be used in legal contexts: нет доста́точно да́нных для возбужде́ния уголо́вного пресле́дования 'there is not enough evidence to prosecute'. The word ули́ки means proof of guilt; cf. the verb улича́ть (уличи́ть) 'to convict': also used in a general sense уличи́ть кого́-либо во лжи 'to find someone out in a lie'. [9] Say 'of such . . . as' (plural).
[10] *R.S.* 42. Probably here the dative construction is the more apt. 'Hypocrisy' cannot be used in the plural in Russian.
[11] зака́тывание глаз.
[12] еле́йные причу́ды. Cf. from the same root чуда́к 'an eccentric'.
[13] уви́ливать (увильну́ть) от (with gen.). This word has the same sense of avoiding by craftiness as the English 'dodge'; cf. уви́ливать от отве́тственности 'to shirk responsibility'.
[14] Use the verb поддава́ться.

# 76

No sooner had the news of[1] Napoleon's escape reached Vienna than the plenipotentiaries of the eight leading powers there assembled declared him an outlaw, and soon afterwards Great Britain, Russia, Austria, and Prussia bound themselves each to put 150,000 men into the field[2] and to keep them under arms 'until Bonaparte should have been rendered absolutely incapable[3] of stirring up further trouble'. Nevertheless Napoleon was not without hope that he might detach Austria and England from the ring[4] of his enemies. He knew that extreme tension over the destinies[5] of Poland and Saxony had arisen at the congress of Vienna[6] between Prussia and Russia on the one hand, and Austria, England, and France on the other, and though the question had been adjusted,[7] he might reasonably expect[8] that the feeling of resentment and suspicion would remain. To Austria, therefore, and Great Britain he addressed letters protesting his desire to keep the peace and his acquiescence in[9] the restricted frontiers of France. His word was not accepted by either ruler. Indeed, had there ever been a chance that Austria would alter her mind, that chance was dispelled in April, when Joachim Murat, acting on his own initiative, broke out of Naples and invaded the Papal States,[10] calling upon the Italian nation to revolt and to accept him as king[11] of a united Italy.

H. A. L. FISHER

[1] извéстие or весть (вéсти) о but not нóвость in this sense of 'tidings about'.

[2] вы́ставить, used absolutely.

[3] покá у Бонапáрта не бýдет отнятá вся́кая возмóжность . . .

[4] вырывáть (вы́рвать) из кольцá. The verb разъединя́ть (разъедини́ть) is not followed by из/от, but by с + instr. in the meaning of 'to disconnect one thing from another'.

[5] напряжéние в связи́ с судьбáми . . .

[6] Remember to make an adjective from Vienna. *R.S.* 152 (i).

[7] вопрóс был улáжен.

[8] Do not use разýмно in parenthesis (мог разýмно ожидáть), but only as part of the impersonal construction бы́ло бы разýмно ожидáть. It is much better, however, to say он мог с основáнием рассчи́тывать на то, что . . .

[9] егó готóвность примири́ться с . . .

[10] пáпская óбласть.

[11] призывáя . . . к восстáнию и к признáнию егó королём . . .

## 77

A conference on the political future of British Guiana began in London yesterday.[1] The Colonial Secretary's opening address struck a cautious note:[2] but it is encouraging and even remarkable that such a conference is meeting at all.[3] When one recalls[4] the dreadful crash with which British Guiana's first essay in[5] representative government ended one must be thankful that so much lost ground has been regained[6]—thankful in particular to the late Governor and to Dr. Jagan, the deposed Premier, for the way in which they have worked together since elected members re-entered the legislative and executive councils two and a half years ago. It would be wrong to think that Dr. Jagan and his colleagues have become 'moderates' in the sense of abating their high hopes for[7] British Guiana's self-government and social development. He holds now that the country is ripe for[8] full self-government, and shrewdly points to the precedent[9] of Cyprus, which has almost exactly the same population—a little over half a million. He has not, in his new capacity as Minister of Trade and Industry, been able to raise all the capital[10] he would like to put into developing[11] his country's resources, but a good deal has been raised and invested; British Guiana has climbed out of the slough[12] in which she lay a dozen years ago, though she has not gone ahead as well as[13] Jamaica and Trinidad. The conference may well decide to return to fully representative government. But it will have to keep an eye on economic responsibilities too.

*The Guardian, 8 March 1960*

[1] The natural Russian word order here is time, place, verb, noun.
[2] Say 'caution sounded in'. [3] вообще́.
[4] е́сли вспо́мнить. For this use of the infinitive see *R.S.* 403.
[5] Say 'attempt to create' попы́тка созда́ть.
[6] Perhaps the best equivalent would be так мно́го из потéрянного удало́сь верну́ть.
[7] что они́ умéрили свои́ упова́ния на. The noun for 'moderates' is the past participle passive of this verb.
[8] Use the verb созрева́ть (созрéть) для. [9] примéр.
[10] срéдства would be appropriate here in combination with добыва́ть (добы́ть).
[11] Say 'to invest (вложи́ть) for the development'.
[12] вы́карабкалась из о́мута. The verb suggests 'extricating oneself from a difficult position'.
[13] не шагну́ла так же далеко́ вперёд как preserves the flavour of the English.

# 78

All things are moving at the same moment. Year by year, month by month, they have all been moving forward together. While we have reached certain positions in thought,[1] others have reached certain positions in fact. The danger is now very near, and a great part of Europe is to a very large extent mobilized. Millions of men are being prepared for war. Everywhere the frontier defences are being manned.[2] Everywhere it is felt that some new stroke is impending. If it should fall,[3] can there be any doubt that we should be involved? We are no longer where we were two or three months ago. We have committed ourselves in every direction,[4] rightly in my opinion, having regard to all that has happened. It is not necessary to enumerate the countries to which directly or indirectly we have given or are giving guarantees. What we should not have dreamt of doing[5] a year ago, when all was so much more powerful, what we should not have dreamt of doing even a month ago, we are doing now. Surely then when we aspire to lead all Europe back from the verge of the abyss on to the uplands[6] of law[7] and peace we must ourselves set the highest example. We must keep nothing back.[8] How can we bear to continue to lead our comfortable, easy lives[9] here at home, unwilling to pronounce even the word 'compulsion', unwilling to take even the necessary measure by which the armies which we have promised can alone[10] be recruited and equipped?[11]

W. S. CHURCHILL

[1] иде́йные пози́ции. One might bring out the difference between abstract and concrete positions by varying the verb used to translate 'reached': e.g. мы утверди́лись на . . . иде́йных пози́циях, други́е за́няли . . . факти́ческие пози́ции.

[2] Use the verb укомплекто́вываться (укомплектова́ться).

[3] е́сли он гря́нет (if уда́р is the subject).

[4] i.e. 'bound ourselves by obligations': мы связа́ли себя́ во всех направле́ниях.

[5] (де́йствия) о кото́рых мы и не помышля́ли бы . . . Notice помышля́ть (помы́слить) to translate 'dream about' in the sense of 'think about in our dreams'; and also the particle и.

[6] высо́ты.

[7] i.e. 'lawfulness', 'legality': правово́й поря́док.

[8] 'To go all out' may be idiomatically rendered by the phrase идти́ на всё.

[9] Say о́браз жи́зни.

[10] Say 'without which . . . cannot . . .'.

[11] не мóгут быть нáбраны и вооружены́ (снабжены́). Note the stresses, and also the various uses of набирáть (набрáть): e.g. — нóмер 'dial a 'phone number'; — скóрость 'pick up speed'; — высотý 'gain height' (of an aeroplane); — пóлный комплéкт 'collect a full set'.

# 79

The Vernon Hotel at which the Twelve True[1] Fishermen[2] held their annual dinners was an institution such as can only exist in an oligarchical society which has gone mad on[3] good manners. It paid[4] not by attracting people but rather by turning people away. In the heart of a plutocracy tradesmen become cunning enough to be[5] more fastidious than their customers. They create difficulties so that their wealthy and weary[6] clients[7] may spend time and money in overcoming them.[8] If there were a fashionable hotel in London which no man could enter[9] who was under six foot, society[10] would meekly make up parties of six-foot men to dine in it.[11] If there were an expensive restaurant which by a mere caprice of its proprietor was open[9] only on Thursday afternoon, it would be crowded[12] on a Thursday afternoon. The Vernon Hotel stood in the corner of a square in Belgravia. It was a small hotel; and a very inconvenient one. But its very inconveniences were considered as walls protecting a particular class. One inconvenience in particular was held to be of vital importance; the fact that only twenty-four people could dine in the place at once. The only big dinner table stood in the open air, on a veranda overlooking[13] one of the most exquisite old gardens in London. Thus it happened that even the twenty-four seats at this table could only be enjoyed in[14] warm weather; and this, making the enjoyment yet more difficult[15] made it yet more desired. The existing owner of the hotel was a Jew named Lever; and he made nearly a million out of it by making it difficult to get into.[16]

G. K. CHESTERTON

[1] A good word here is и́стый, which means 'true' in the sense of 'zealous', 'devoted', e.g. и́стый библиофи́л 'a true lover of books'.

[2] рыба́к means 'one who fishes for a living'. The correct word here is рыболо́в 'angler'.

[3] помеша́вшийся (or поме́шанный) на хоро́шем то́не.

[4] дава́л при́быль or окупа́лся.

[5] Say 'show great cunning and become'.

[6] Perhaps пресы́щенные жи́знью.

[7] A number of different words have to be found in this piece with the general meaning of 'customer'; завсегда́тай 'habitué' offers an acceptable variation.

[8] Say 'on their overcoming'.

[9] These verbs are contrary to fact and will therefore be subjunctives.

[10] Say 'higher society'.

[11] Say 'arrange dinners there, assembling at them exclusively people six foot tall'.

[12] A possible verb to use here is ломи́ться от 'to be crammed with'; cf. по́лки ло́мятся от книг 'the shelves are crammed with books'. Alternatives are перепо́лнен до отка́за or битко́м наби́т.

[13] выходи́вший в (not на).

[14] в (and acc.).

[15] The verb затрудня́ть (затрудни́ть) has precisely the sense required here—'to make difficult through the creation of obstacles'. The corresponding adjective затрудни́тельный means 'girt with difficulties'; cf. тру́дный, which means simply 'difficult to solve'.

[16] Say 'through the fact that (тем, что) he made access to it extremely difficult' (see previous note).

## 80

There has appeared in our time a particular class of books[1] which I sincerely and solemnly think may be called the silliest[2] ever known among men. They are much more wild[3] than the wildest romances of chivalry and much more dull than the dullest religious tract. Moreover, the romances of chivalry were at least about chivalry; the religious tracts are about religion. But[4] these things are about nothing; they are about what is called Success. On every bookstall, in every magazine you will find works telling people how to succeed.[5] They are books showing men how to succeed in everything; they are written by men who cannot even succeed in writing[6] books. To begin with,[7] of course, there is no such thing as Success. Or, if you like to put it so, there is nothing that is not successful.[8] That a thing is successful merely means that it is;[9] a millionaire is successful in being a millionaire and a donkey in being a donkey. Any live man has succeeded in living; any dead man may have succeeded in committing suicide. But, passing over the bad logic and bad philosophy in the phrase, we may take it, as these writers do, as meaning success in obtaining money or worldly position. These writers profess to tell[10] the ordinary man how he may succeed in his trade or speculation—how, if he is a builder, he may succeed as a builder; how, if he is a stockbroker, he may succeed as a stockbroker.

G. K. CHESTERTON

[1] Say 'books of a particular kind'.

[2] *R.S.* 514 (i). To express in Russian this substantival use of an English adjective, it is often best to repeat the preceding noun. Say 'the silliest of all books ever created'.

[3] экстравага́нтный.

[4] Use же. *R.S.* 422 (i).

[5] Use the simple verb преуспе́ть.

[6] Say 'the writing of'.

[7] Нача́ть хотя́ бы с того́, что.

[8] Say 'that is not success'. *R.S.* 267.

[9] Say 'Saying that this or that has succeeded, we mean that it simply exists'.

[10] Perhaps притяза́ют объясня́ть.

## 81

And now for the first time my courage completely failed[1] me. It is enough to say that I was penniless, and a prisoner in a foreign country, where I had no friend,[2] nor any knowledge of the customs or language of the people. I was at the mercy of men with whom I had little in common. And yet, engrossed as I was[3] with my extremely difficult and doubtful[4] position, I could not help feeling deeply interested in the people among whom I had fallen. What was the meaning of that room full of old machinery which I had just seen,[5] and of the displeasure with which the magistrate had regarded my watch? The people had very little machinery now. I had been struck with this over and over again, though I had not been more than four-and-twenty hours in the country. They were about as far advanced as Europeans of the twelfth or thirteenth century; certainly not more so.[6] And yet they must have had at one time the fullest knowledge of our own most recent inventions. How could it have happened that having been once so far in advance[7] they were now as much behind[7] us? It was evident that it was not from ignorance. They knew my watch as a watch when they saw it;[8] and the care with which the broken machines were preserved and ticketed,[9] proved that they had not lost the recollection of their former civilization.

SAMUEL BUTLER

[1] Use the verb измени́ть.
[2] Plural in Russian.
[3] Say 'although I was engrossed in thoughts of'.
[4] двусмы́сленный, неопределённый.
[5] Begin a new sentence here. 'Why had the magistrate . . . .'
[6] Re-cast this sentence. Say 'had reached the cultural level, let us say, of Europeans of the twelfth or thirteenth century, not more'.
[7] Use two single verbs in Russian.
[8] с пе́рвого взгля́да.
[9] отме́ченные ярлыка́ми.

## 82

In the stories written in the second half of the fifties and the early sixties Tolstoy's centre of interest is shifted from analysis to morality. These stories—*The Memoirs of a Billiard Marker*, *Two Hussars*, *Albert*, *Lucerne*, *Three Deaths*,

*Family Happiness*, *Polikushka* and *Kholstomer*, *the Story of a Horse*—are frankly[1] didactic and moralistic, much more so than any of the stories of his last dogmatic period. The main moral of these stories is the fallacy[2] of civilization and the inferiority[3] of the civilized, conscious, sophisticated man, with his artificially[4] multiplied needs, to natural man. On the whole they mark an advance neither in Tolstoy's method of annexing and digesting[5] reality, nor in his skill in transferring the raw experience of life into art.[6] Most of them are crude and some (as, for instance, *Three Deaths*) did not need a Tolstoy to write them. Contemporary criticism was right in regarding them if not as a decline, at least as a standstill[7] in the development of his genius. But they are important as an expression of that moral urge[8] which was finally to bring Tolstoy to *A Confession* and to all his later work and teaching. *Lucerne*, for its earnest and bitter indignation against the selfishness of the rich (which, it is true, Tolstoy was inclined to regard, semi-Slavophilwise, as a peculiarity of the materialistic civilization of the West) is particularly suggestive of the spirit of his later work. As a sermon in fiction[9] it is certainly one of the most powerful things of its kind. The nearest approach to complete artistic success is *Two Hussars*, a charming story that betrays its purpose[10] only in the excessively neat parallelism between the characters of the two hussars, father and son.

D. S. MIRSKY

[1] Omit 'frankly' and transpose 'much more'.

[2] Expand to 'an assertion of the fallacy'.

[3] There is no single Russian word for 'inferiority'. Say 'superiority' and make the necessary changes.

[4] Use the adjective наду́манный.

[5] переосмы́слить.

[6] Say 'communicating . . . in artistic form'.

[7] засто́й.

[8] Say 'seeking'.

[9] Say 'given in the form of a work of fiction'.

[10] Say 'the true purpose of which is revealed'.

## 83

Those who occupied the gallery, to whom this offensive and impolite speech was addressed, were the family of Cedric the Saxon, with that of his ally and kinsman, Athelstane of Coningsburgh, a personage who, on account of[1] his descent from the last Saxon monarchs of England, was held in the highest respect by[2] all the Saxon natives of the north of England. But with the blood of this ancient royal race[3] many of their infirmities had descended to[4] Athelstane. He was comely in countenance, bulky and strong in person,[5] and in the flower of his age; yet inanimate in expression, dull-eyed, heavy-browed, inactive and sluggish in all his movements, and so slow in resolution,[6] that the soubriquet of one of his ancestors was conferred upon[4] him, and he was very generally called Athelstane the Unready.[7] His friends—and he had many who, as well as Cedric, were passionately attached to him—contended that this sluggish temper arose not from want of courage, but from mere want[8] of decision; others alleged that his hereditary vice of[9] drunkenness had obscured his faculties, never[10] of a very acute order, and that the passive courage and meek good-nature which remained behind were merely the dregs of a character that might have been deserving of praise, but of which all the valuable parts[11] had been destroyed in the progress of a long course of debauchery.

WALTER SCOTT

[1] по [2] Say 'enjoyed the profoundest respect among'.

[3] Perhaps пле́мя короле́й. The archaic flavour of пле́мя suits the style. [4] перейти́ к. [5] *R.S.* 54.

[6] Say 'his expression was lifeless, his eyes dull, his brow heavy, his movements lethargic and indolent, and his character so indecisive that'. Note нахму́ренные бро́ви. [7] Ательстэ́н Ме́шкотный.

[8] Say 'solely from'. 'Solely' may be well translated by еди́нственно.

[9] Omit. [10] и без того́ не.

[11] Say 'if only all his good qualities had not been'. 'Good' in Russian might be stylistically qualified by the adverb ско́лько-нибу́дь 'at all'.

# 84

A tall, thin old man, who, however, had lost by the habit of stooping much of his actual height, approached the lower end of the table. His features, keen and regular, with an aquiline nose, and piercing black eyes, his high, wrinkled forehead and long grey hair and beard might have been considered as handsome,[1] had they not been the marks of a physiognomy peculiar to a race which, during those dark ages,[2] was alike detested by the credulous and prejudiced vulgar[3] and persecuted by the greedy and rapacious nobility.

The Jew's dress, which appeared to have suffered considerably from the storm, was a plain russet cloak of[4] many folds covering a dark purple tunic. He had large boots lined with[5] fur and a belt around his waist from[6] which hung a small knife together with a case of[7] writing materials, but no weapon. He wore a high, square yellow cap of a peculiar fashion which he doffed with great humility at the door of[8] the hall.

The reception of[9] this person in the hall of Cedric the Saxon was such as might have satisfied[10] the most prejudiced enemy of the tribes of Israel. Cedric himself coldly nodded in answer to[11] the Jew's repeated greetings and signed to him to take a place[12] at the lower end of the table, where, however, no one offered to make room[13] for him. On the contrary, as he passed along the file,[14] casting a timid, supplicating glance towards each of those who occupied the lower end of the table, the Saxon servants squared their shoulders[15] and continued eating their supper, paying not the slightest attention to the new guest.

WALTER SCOTT

[1] Say 'gave him an agreeable appearance' and follow with 'but on them lay the mark of . . .'.

[2] невéжественные векá. *R.S.* 533 (iii).

[3] чернь is a good word here. [4] Say 'with'.
[5] 'To line with' подбить (+ instr.). [6] Say 'on'.
[7] Say 'with'. [8] Say 'at the entrance to'. *R.S.* 564.
[9] Say 'extended to' оказанный.
[10] Say simply 'might have satisfied'. [11] на.
[12] Say 'indicated a place to him'. [13] посторониться.
[14] Say 'passed by those sitting'.
[15] сдвигались плечами or расправляли плечи.

# 85

By six o'clock, the queue for the unreserved seats already stretched[1] a quarter of a mile down the road. At seven, the commissionaire went out, counted them, compared their number with the seats available,[2] and informed those who would be unable to get in[3] of the uselessness of waiting. The latter part[4] of the queue broke up[5] and dissipated, but a great many of its members continued to wait about, partly in order to see any celebrities who might be recognizable,[6] partly in the hope that some of the reserved seats might not be claimed[7] and that they might still be able to get in. Three policemen inefficiently but self-importantly[8] regulated the increasing flow of people. Even those who had booked seats arrived early to claim them, fearful of not getting in, and having done so, hung about[9] in small knots on the lawns in front, chattering excitedly. From every hotel in Oxford came agents, theatrical managers, actors, actresses, producers, critics, and fellow-playwrights. Some, who[10] had not been able to leave town earlier on account of business, came direct from the station in taxicabs. The intelligentsia of the university arrived with habitual expressions[11] of boredom. Dons arrived and made their way in with the practised ease[12] and tranquillity of those in authority. Everywhere there was talk, talk, talk. A group of three eminent critics stood outside, talking spasmodically[13] and glancing nervously over their shoulders.

EDMUND CRISPIN

1 The verb in Russian must be followed by a preposition. *R.S.* 656 (vii). 2 *R.S.* 326 (i). 3 попа́сть.

4 Say 'The tail'.

5 рассе́ялся or распа́лся.

6 Say 'whom it would be possible to recognize'.

7 Say 'for some of the reserved seats they (impersonal) would not come'.

8 Say 'with a feeling of their own importance'.

9 Use the verb окола́чиваться.

10 Drop 'Some' and say simply Те, кто.

11 Singular in Russian.

12 Perhaps с привы́чной уве́ренностью. 13 уры́вками.

# 86

It was[1] because I felt this that Dirk Stroeve was not to me, as to others, merely an object of ridicule. His fellow-painters made no secret of their contempt for his work, but he earned a fair amount[2] of money, and they did not hesitate[3] to make free use of[4] his purse. He was generous, and the needy, laughing at him because he believed[5] so naïvely their stories of distress, borrowed from him with effrontery. He was very emotional, yet his feeling, so easily aroused, had in it something absurd, so that you accepted his kindness, but felt no gratitude.[6] To take[7] money from him was like[8] robbing a child, and you despised him because he was so foolish. I imagine that a pickpocket, proud of his light fingers,[9] must feel a sort of indignation with[10] the careless woman who leaves in a cab a vanity-bag with all her jewels in it. Nature had made him a butt, but had denied him insensibility. He writhed under the jokes, which were perpetually made[11] at his expense, and yet never ceased, it seemed wilfully, to expose himself to them. He was constantly wounded, and yet his good-nature was such that he could not bear malice.

W. SOMERSET MAUGHAM

1 Begin with и́менно.

2 прили́чные за́работки 'a decent salary'. The adverb прили́чно may also be used, with the appropriate verb.

[3] Work in без вся́кого стесне́ния.

[4] The verb распоряжа́ться (распоряди́ться) 'to use', 'to dispose of', is very commonly used of money (+ instr.).

[5] принима́л на ве́ру.

[6] Say 'his kindness evoked no feeling of gratitude'.

[7] The infinitive here makes a statement of general principle. *R.S.* 222. [8] всё равно́, что. [9] Say 'the dexterity of his hands'.

[10] Say 'when some woman or other carelessly leaves'.

[11] Work in the expression осыпа́ть насме́шками.

## 87

Now a policeman, I am sorry to say, cannot be a perfectly civilized human being. Those who use authority,[1] like those who create wealth,[2] can be civilized but not completely civilized. They must be of the second order.[3] The mere exercise of power,[4] the coercing of others, will tinge a man[5] with barbarism. My praetorians, my policemen, my administrators and magistrates, and I myself—if I am to be an efficient[6] ruler, which, however, I decline to be[7]—must be content to be the imperfectly civilized guardians of civility. Fortunately, there are in the world a number of people who appear not only to enjoy ruling (an all too common taste), but to enjoy ruling well. These also are the instruments of civilization. They had rather rule well than ill; and if in fact they generally fail that is the result not of malevolence but of stupidity. It should not be impossible for[8] a civilized élite[9] by bringing intelligence and education into fashion[10] partially to remedy this; and if I were a highly civilized Hindoo that would be my plan. Gladly I should leave to high-minded young Englishmen the dirty work[11] of governing; but I should try by hook or by crook to make the high-minded young Englishmen a little brighter in their heads.[12]

CLIVE BELL

[1] Perhaps власть иму́щие, though somewhat ironical, would be appropriate here. [2] Use бога́тство in the plural (cf. 'riches').

[3] принадлежа́ть к числу́ второразря́дных люде́й.

[4] облада́ние вла́стью (see *R.S.* 47), while being the nearest idiomatic Russian stock expression, does not necessarily suggest use as well as possession: perhaps therefore say примене́ние вла́сти. 'The mere' уже́ само́.

[5] Say 'imparts to man a tint' придаёт . . . отте́нок.

[6] A difficult word; компете́нтный means 'qualified', 'expert'; делово́й or де́льный better convey the sense of 'businesslike' or 'efficient'.

[7] каковы́м . . . я отка́зываюсь быть.

[8] To avoid the cumbersome literal rendering не должно́ бы́ло бы быть, make a positive statement of it. Continue with для + gen. and an infinitive.

[9] цвет о́бщества.

[10] сде́лав мо́дными . . . is one possible rendering.

[11] чёрная рабо́та.

[12] научи́ть . . . немно́го бо́льше шевели́ть мозга́ми (a common colloquial expression for 'to use one's brains').

## 88

Greek and Roman society was built on the conception[1] of the subordination[2] of the individual to the community, of the citizen to the state; it set the safety of the commonwealth, as the supreme aim of conduct,[3] above the safety of the individual whether in this world or in a world to come.[4] Trained from infancy in this unselfish ideal,[5] the citizens devoted their lives to the public service[6] and were ready to lay them down for the common good; or, if they shrank from the supreme sacrifice, it never occurred to them that they acted otherwise than basely in preferring[7] their personal existence to the interests of their country. All this was changed by the spread of Oriental religions which inculcated[8] the communion[9] of the soul with God and its eternal salvation as the only objects worth living for, objects in comparison with which the prosperity and even the existence of the state sank into insignificance. The inevitable result of this selfish and immoral doctrine was to withdraw[10] the devotee more and more from the public service, to concentrate[10] his thoughts on his own spiritual emotions, and to breed[10] in him a contempt for the present life, which he regarded merely as a probation for[11] a better and an eternal. The saint and the recluse, disdainful of earth and rapt in ecstatic contemplation of heaven,[12] became in popular opinion the highest ideal of humanity, displacing[13] the old ideal of the patriot and hero who, forgetful of self, lives and is ready to die for the good of his country.

J. G. FRAZER

[1] Say 'At the basis . . . lay the conception' (в осно́ве... лежа́ло поня́тие).

[2] подчинённость suggests the state of being subordinate, and is perhaps preferable here to подчине́ние.

[3] A difficult phrase. Perhaps как верхо́вную но́рму поведе́ния.

[4] Use гряду́щий. [5] воспи́танный на э́том . . . идеа́ле.

[6] i.e. the act of serving. *R.S.* 110. [7] Present gerund.

[8] 'Inculcated . . . as . . . .' Here simply учи́ли, что conveys the meaning adequately. [9] In this sense обще́ние.

[10] Make nouns from these three verbs, and make them the joint subjects: после́дствием . . . был всё бо́льший отхо́д . . . сосредото́чение . . . и вы́работка в нём (в них) . . . See also *R.S.* 23.

[11] иску́с is perhaps the best word for 'probation' in this sense (in the meaning of 'temptation' it is now archaic), but it is normally used absolutely. To translate the preposition 'for', some periphrasis is necessary, e.g. как иску́с, как перехо́д к лу́чшей . . . жи́зни.

[12] Possible versions are восто́рженно созерца́ющие ра́йские мисте́рии or погружённые в исступлённое созерца́ние небе́с.

[13] Use past gerund.

## 89

The snow has only just stopped, and in the court below my rooms[1] all sounds are dulled.[2] There were few sounds to hear,[3] for it was early in January, and the college was empty and quiet;[4] I could just make out the footsteps of the porter, as he passed beneath the window on his last round of the night.[5] Now and again[6] his keys clinked,[7] and the clink[7] reached me after the pad[8] of his footsteps had been lost in the snow.

I had drawn my curtains early that evening and not moved out. The kitchens[9] had sent up a meal, and I had eaten it as I read[10] by the fire. It was scorchingly hot in front of the fire, and warm, cosy, shielded,[11] in the zone of the two armchairs and the sofa which formed an island of comfort round the fireplace. Outside that zone, as one went towards[12] the walls of the lofty medieval room, the draughts were bitter. In a blaze of firelight, which shone into the sombre corners, the panelling on the walls glowed softly,[13] almost rosily, but no warmth reached as far. So that, on a night like this, one came to treat most of the room as the open air, and hurried back to the cosy island in front of the fireplace, the pool of light[14] from the reading lamp on the mantelpiece, the radiance[15] which was more pleasant because of the cold air which one had just escaped.

I was comfortable in my armchair, relaxed and content.[16] There was no need to move. I was reading so intently that I did not notice[17] the steps on the staircase, until there came a quick repeated knock on my door, and Jago came in.

C. P. SNOW

[1] Say 'under my window(s)'. [2] приглушены́.
[3] впро́чем зву́ков бы́ло немно́го. [4] *R.S.* 159.
[5] ночно́й обхо́д. [6] *R.S.* 197 (ii).
[7] The prefix по- and the suffix -ива are added to the root verb звя́кать to form a new imperfective verb позвя́кивать 'to clink now and again', which gives the exact sense required here. See *R.S.* 246. There is also a noun позвя́кивание. [8] Say simply звук.
[9] Say 'From the kitchen they (impersonal) had sent me . . .'
[10] Say 'by the fire, not ceasing to read'.
[11] бы́ло . . . защищено́.
[12] The impersonal flavour can be preserved by the use of е́сли + the infinitive: е́сли направля́ться к . . . See *R.S.* 403.
[13] A possible translation is в отсве́те ками́нного пла́мени, озаря́вшего тёмные углы́, стенны́е пане́ли освеща́лись мя́гко . . .
[14] сноп све́та is perhaps the nearest equivalent.
[15] Say simply 'warmth'.
[16] я чу́вствовал себя́ отдохну́вшим и дово́льным.
[17] Use the perfective verb расслы́шать.

## 90

In attempting to reach[1] the genuine psychological reason for the popularity of detective stories, it is necessary to rid ourselves of many mere[2] phrases. It is not true, for example, that the populace prefer bad literature to good, and accept detective stories because they are bad literature. The mere absence of artistic subtlety does not make a book popular.[3] Bradshaw's *Railway Guide* contains few gleams[4] of psychological comedy, yet it is not read aloud uproariously[5] on winter evenings. If detective stories are read with more exuberance than railway guides, it is certainly because they are more artistic. Many good books have fortunately been popular; many bad books, still more fortunately,[6] have been unpopular. A good detective story would probably be even more popular than a bad one. The trouble in this matter is that many people do not realize that there is such a thing as a good detective story; it is to them like speaking of a good[7] devil. To write a story about a burglary is, in their eyes, a sort of spiritual manner of committing it.[8] To persons of somewhat weak sensibility[9] this is natural enough; it must be confessed that many detective stories are as full of[10] sensational crime as one[11] of Shakespeare's plays.

There is, however, between a good detective story and a bad detective story as much, or, rather more, difference than there is between a good epic and a bad one. Not only is a detective story a perfectly legitimate form of art, but it has certain definite and real advantages as an agent of the public weal.[12]

G. K. CHESTERTON

[1] установи́ть. [2] Perhaps here пусто́й.

[3] *R.S.* 37 (i). [4] про́блески.

[5] под взры́вы сме́ха is a good rendering. For similar uses of под + acc., meaning 'to the accompaniment of', see *R.S.* 681.

[6] If к сча́стью is used, as it normally is, to translate the simple adverb, the comparative cannot be translated by the same expression

prefaced by ещё бо́лее. One occasionally meets к ещё бо́льшему сча́стью, although it may be safer here to render the meaning rather freely by some such phrase as и э́то ещё важне́е.

7 то же са́мое, что говори́ть о добродетельном чёрте.

8 В их глаза́х написа́ть расска́з о грабеже́ э́то вро́де как мы́сленно соверши́ть его́.

9 Say 'For people with rather weak nerves'.

10 во мно́гих . . . сто́лько же . . . ско́лько . . .

11 i.e. 'as any one' любо́й.

12 как ору́дие общественного бла́га or simply для о́бщего бла́га.

# 91

It would not, I think, be doing justice to[1] the feelings which are uppermost in many of our hearts[2] if we passed to the business of the day without taking notice[3] of the fresh gap[4] which has been made in our ranks by the untimely death of Mr. Alfred Lyttelton. It is a loss of which I hardly trust myself[5] to speak, for apart from ties of relationship,[6] there has subsisted between us for thirty-three years a close friendship and affection which no political differences were ever allowed to loosen or even to affect. Nor can I better describe it than by saying[7] that he, perhaps, of all men of this generation came nearest the ideal of manhood which every English father would like to see his son aspire to and if possible attain.[8] Body, mind, and character—the schoolroom, the cricket field, the Bar, the House of Commons—each made its separate contribution to[9] the faculties and the experience of a many-sided and harmonious whole. But what he was he gave.[10] He was as we here know a strenuous fighter. He has left behind him no resentments and no enmity; nothing but a gracious memory[11] for a manly and winning personality—the memory of one who served with an unstinted measure of devotion his generation and his country.

H. H. ASQUITH

1 If the impersonal form (несправедли́во) is retained, it may be followed by по отноше́нию к; otherwise make a personal construction using the phrase отдава́ть (отда́ть) справедли́вость + dat.

[2] Say 'in the hearts of many of us'.
[3] Negative past gerund. [4] брешь.
[5] едва́ осме́ливаюсь. [6] ро́дственные свя́зи.
[7] и я лу́чше не могу́ описа́ть э́то, чем сказа́в . . .
[8] When two verbs governing different constructions (стреми́ться к, дости́гнуть + gen.) follow one another in a context such as this, the relative pronoun should go in the case required by the first verb, e.g. к кото́рой (кото́рому) ка́ждый . . . оте́ц хоте́л бы, что́бы сын его́ стреми́лся, и, е́сли возмо́жно, дости́г.
[9] все́ э́то — ка́ждое в отде́льности — спосо́бствовало . . .
[10] Two possible translations are: он дава́л всё, что в нём бы́ло; and он дава́л всего́ себя́.
[11] The adjective combined most commonly with па́мять in contexts of this sort is све́тлая (continue: о + prep.—'memory for').

## 92

Anyone who[1] is concerned,[2] as I am, with the development of Britain's export trade,[3] must be struck at once by the contrast between the size, strength, and rapid[4] development of the Soviet economy on the one hand, and by the relatively small flow of trade between Russia and the United Kingdom on the other. The United Kingdom sells barely 1 per cent. of its exports to the Soviet Union, and we buy less than two per cent. of our imports from them. Must this contrast continue?[5] Is there not[6] a valuable untapped[7] market here for British goods which our firms can develop?

Of course, no one thinks that the Soviet Union will wish to abandon its now traditional aim of building up home production[8] of many things which might be obtained elsewhere. But if the Russians are now impressed with the advantages of international trade, and are ready gradually to expand their commercial contacts with the West, they will find us ready partners.[9] Indeed they know that British business men are anxious to grasp the opportunities offered to them.[10] British exports to Russia were[11] about ten million pounds in 1954, and rose as high as thirty-seven millions in 1957. In 1960 we may have exceeded this figure.

Her Majesty's Government have welcomed this development of trade and we have done what we can to encourage it. In the first place we have reduced[12] to quite small proportions the list of goods which may not be exported to the Soviet Union for strategic reasons.[13] Although goods of military and quasi-military value are still restricted,[14] we believe that the list does not now prevent the growth of a broadly based commerce.

*The Guardian*

[1] Say 'All those who'. *R.S.* 474.

[2] заинтересо́ван в (+ prep.). The verb заинтересо́вывать (заинтересова́ть) may have one of two meanings: 'to arouse the interest of', меня́ заинтересова́ло но́вое представле́ние *Трёх сестёр*; 'to interest materially', мы, как зде́шние поме́щики, заинтересо́ваны в э́том де́ле.

[3] The nouns и́мпорт and э́кспорт may mean either 'the act of importing and exporting (ввоз, вы́воз), total imports (exports)' or 'import (export) trade'. Cf. бросово́й (or бро́совый) э́кспорт 'dumping'.

[4] Say 'the broad, strong, and rapid economic development'.

[5] One possibility here is to use the verb мири́ться (примири́ться) с which means 'to accept something bad'. With the perfective form помири́ться it means 'to become reconciled after estrangement', поссо́рившиеся друзья́ помири́лись.

[6] *R.S.* 326 (i).

[7] нетро́нутый.

[8] Say 'production at home' (у себя́).

[9] Say 'then they can count on our readiness to co-operate in every way in this direction'.

[10] представля́ющиеся им торго́вые возмо́жности.

[11] Use the verb равня́ться.

[12] In this sense of 'curtailing', сократи́ть. Cf. сократи́ть расхо́ды.

[13] из стратеги́ческих соображе́ний.

[14] Say 'there are still a number of restrictions on the export of'.

## 93

Mr. Khrushchev's visit to[1] Indonesia, which ended last week, has left a number of mysteries behind. During the tour it came out that he had invited himself. For a part[2] of the time he was in less than[3] his ordinary good humour, and the tour evidently did not go entirely as he wanted. He and his hosts disputed about the terms[4] of the final communiqué: it omitted[5] some polite references to China which Mr. Khrushchev wanted in, presumably because he desires to keep formally on good terms with China, and which the Indonesians wanted out because they are currently quarrelling with China.

One of Mr. Khrushchev's objects may have been to reassert[6] Russian influence in South-East Asia, and to replace Chinese authority over[7] the Indonesian Communist Party by Russian authority. But Peking Radio was very cold at[8] this Russian foray into the Far East, and China may be equally dubious about[8] Russia's economic offers to Indonesia.

Mr. Khrushchev's manœuvres against China—if that is what they were[9]—were behind the scenes. His manœuvres against the West were open. His speeches in India and Indonesia showed that he interprets competitive co-existence as meaning out-and-out[10] competition between Russia and the West, stopping short of war.[10] On every possible occasion he recalled Asia's past wrongs, and begged Asians to look the present Western gift horses in the mouth. Russian aid, he inferred, was going to be quite different from Western aid. But he did not explain how Russian aid, which has to be[11] repaid and is given on fairly stiff terms,[12] is going to prove more beneficial than American, which is often gratis.

*The Observer*

[1] *R.S.* 29 (i). [2] Omit 'for'. [3] Say 'not quite in'.

[4] Use язы́к. [5] Say 'in it were omitted'.

[6] Use nouns: одно́й из це́лей ... могло́ быть восстановле́ние ... и заме́на ... [7] If авторите́т is used, continue with в, not над.

[8] In both cases use относи́ться and the appropriate adverb.

[9] е́сли их так мо́жно назва́ть.

[10] Combine the two and say 'competition by all means with the exception of (*or* 'only stopping short of') ...'.

[11] Use the future ('which it will be necessary to repay').

[12] на дово́льно тяжёлых усло́виях.

## 94

If Cyprus can in no way, either in architecture or landscape,[1] ever rival Corfu or Italy, yet it would be unfair to deny that Broussa in Asia Minor challenges comparison[2] with them. Motoring to Broussa from the sea, early in the month of May, you pass through an exquisite Italian landscape,[3] the lines of newly leafed[4] poplars with their glittering golden discs distilling odours of balsam into the already redolent air of the spring.[5] And Broussa itself, when you come to it, proves to be a small city of neat, strict, and relevant[6] beauty. However, you are soon disabused of the comparison as you first perceive the minarets and mosques. They are architectural works of delicacy and imagination,[7] more in the style of Persia than of Turkey, and they contain wonderful tiles of blue and green. On a lower scale, Broussa further resembles an Italian city[8] in that its neighbourhood produces a delicate white wine, delicious to drink on the spot but which will not travel.[9] Of an orange-yellow colour, it is made—since Mohammedans are forbidden to drink fermented liquor—by an agricultural colony of Jews long settled here. . . . From Broussa we motored one afternoon to the Bithynian Mount Olympus. Though it was late spring, the snow still lay on the upper slopes. Indeed, as we regarded it,[10] one snow-field began to melt under the rays of the hot sun, to reveal at its edges huge patches of blue scilla in full flower.

OSBERT SITWELL

[1] Say 'beauty of nature'.

[2] Use the expression напра́шиваться на сравне́ние с. The verb напра́шиваться (напроси́ться) translates a number of English idioms; cf. напроси́ться на комплиме́нты 'to fish for compliments', напроси́ться на неприя́тности 'to ask for trouble'.

[3] Say италья́нские пейза́жи.

[4] Cf. то́лько-что распусти́вшиеся ли́пы (L. Tolstoy).

[5] Perhaps отяжеле́вший от весе́нних арома́тов во́здух.

[6] гармонúрующей с мéстностью.
[7] тóнкого вкýса и крылáтой фантáзии.
[8] Say 'Italian cities'.
[9] не тéрпящее перевóзки.
[10] Work in the expression на нáших глазáх.

## 95

My pictures are poems in lines. If they are ever able to lay claim to fame, they will do so[1] primarily as a rhythmical expression of form, and not as the interpretation of an idea or the representation of facts.

The universe speaks with but one tongue—the tongue of gestures; its voice is the picture and the dance. Everything in this world states in the dumb language of lines and colours that it is not simply a logical abstraction or a useful object, but that it is unique of its kind[2] and contains within itself the miracle of its existence.

There are a countless number of familiar[3] things which we never regard from the point of view of their true beauty, irrespective of the good or the harm they do.[4] A flower exists as a flower, and that is enough;[5] but at the same time I see in a cigarette only a means of satisfying the habit of smoking. However, there are other things as well, the fact of whose existence we accept by virtue of their dynamic quality.[6] They stand out in the book of creation[7] like lines underscored in coloured pencil. We cannot walk past without noticing them.[8]

The artist creates in his picture the language of indisputable reality, and we are satisfied by[9] the mere contemplation of it. It is not necessarily the portrait of a beautiful woman. It might be the portrait of a donkey or anything else which is not the outward expression of what exists in nature, but which reveals its meaning only through[10] its inner artistic content.

People often ask me about the meaning of my pictures, but I remain as silent as the pictures themselves. They *express*, but they do not *explain*.

RABINDRANATH TAGORE (*adapted*)

N.B. It will be found that most of this passage will go fairly literally into Russian without the need to recast the sentences or to depart much from the original words; e.g. 'lines', 'rhythmical', 'form', 'interpretation', and 'abstraction' all have the same roots in Russian and are in fact borrowings.

[1] If the future tense (смо́гут) is used in the first part of the sentence, it will be sufficient to continue: то пре́жде всего́ как . . .

[2] еди́нственный в своём ро́де.

[3] привы́чных нам.

[4] приноси́ть (принести́) is a useful verb: e.g. приноси́ть по́льзу 'to be of use', 'to do good'; — плоды́ 'to bear fruit'; — удово́льствие 'to give pleasure'.

[5] и э́того доста́точно. See also *R.S.* 397.

[6] Perhaps сво́йственная им дина́мика (in the appropriate case).

[7] творе́ние would be apt in this somewhat rhetorical context.

[8] Negative past gerund.

[9] Use the active voice.

[10] Say 'in'.

## 96

'Ah, realize[1] your youth while you have it. Don't squander the gold of your days,[2] listening to the tedious, trying to improve the hopeless failure,[3] or giving away your life to the ignorant,[4] the common,[4] and the vulgar.[4] These are the sickly aims, the false ideals, of our age. Live! Live the wonderful life[5] that is in you! Let nothing be lost upon you.[6] Be always searching for new sensations. Be afraid of nothing. . . . A new Hedonism—that is what our century wants. You might be its visible symbol. With your personality there is nothing you could not do. The world belongs to you for a season. . . . The moment I met you[7] I saw that you were quite unconscious of what you really are, of what you really might be. There was so much in you that charmed me that I felt I must tell you something about yourself. I thought how tragic it would be if you were wasted. For there is such a little time that your youth will last—such a little time. The common hill-flowers[8] wither, but they blossom again. The laburnum will be as yellow next June as it is now. But we never get back[9] our youth.... Youth! Youth! There is absolutely nothing in the world but youth!'

Dorian Gray listened, open-eyed and wondering.[10] The spray of lilac fell from his hand upon the gravel. A furry[11] bee came and buzzed round it for a moment.... Two green-and-white[12] butterflies fluttered past,[13] and in the pear-tree at the corner of the garden a thrush began to sing.[14]

OSCAR WILDE

[1] Say 'take advantage of' по́льзуйтесь.

[2] This phrase can be translated quite literally.

[3] Perhaps simply the plural adjective безнадёжные, used as a noun.

[4] Use three nouns, e.g. неве́жда, &c..

[5] *R.S.* 52 (iii).

[6] Пусть ничто́ для вас не пропада́ет. See *R.S.* 219 and 521.

[7] Use a prepositional construction: *R.S.* 529.

[8] Say 'the flowers of the field' полевы́е цветы́.

[9] Notice that верну́ть can mean both 'to give back' ('restore') and 'to get back' ('recover').

[10] Say 'having opened his eyes wide (past gerund), listened in wonder' (с удивле́нием). [11] мохна́тый. [12] бе́ло-зелёный.

[13] ми́мо порхну́ли could well start the sentence.

[14] Use the prefix за-.

## 97

The country[1] was the grandest that can be imagined.[2] How often have I sat[3] on the mountain side and watched the waving downs,[4] with the two white specks of huts in the distance, and the little square of garden[5] behind them; the paddock[6] with a patch of bright green oats above the huts, and the yards and wool-sheds[6] down on the flat below; all seen as through the wrong end of a telescope,[7] so clear and brilliant was the air, or as upon a colossal model or map spread out beneath me. Beyond the downs was a plain, going down to a river of great size, on the farther side of which there were other high mountains, with the winter's snow still not quite melted; up the river, which ran winding in[8] many streams over a bed some two miles broad,[9] I looked upon the second great chain, and could see a narrow gorge where the river retired[10] and was lost. I knew that there was a range still farther back; but except from one place[11] near the very top of my own mountain, no part of it was visible. . . . Never shall I forget the utter loneliness of the prospect—only the little faraway homestead giving sign of[12] human handiwork; the vastness of mountain and plain, of river and sky; the marvellous atmospheric effects—sometimes[13] black mountains against a white sky, and then again,[13] after cold weather,[14] white mountains against a black sky—sometimes seen through breaks and swirls of cloud.[15] And sometimes, which was best of all, I went up my mountain in a fog, and then got above the mist; going higher and higher, I would look down upon a sea of whiteness, through which would be thrust[16] innumerable mountain tops that looked like islands.

SAMUEL BUTLER

[1] Here мéстность (or прирóда).

[2] так . . . как тóлько мóжно себé предстáвить. For the idiomatic тóлько see Passage 69, note 8.

[3] Here is an opportunity to use the colloquial iterative verb сúживать (which is never found in the present tense).

[4] Presumably the undulating line of the downs: волнúстая лúния холмóв.

[5] Say 'with two white specks—huts', putting 'huts' (хúжины) in the instrumental case in apposition to 'specks'. Similarly for 'square of garden' say 'square garden'.

[6] Two suggestions are загóн and сарáи для шéрсти respectively.

[7] всё вы́глядело так, сло́вно вы смотре́ли в телеско́п не с того́ конца́. See *R.S.* 183 for the translation of 'wrong'.

[8] текла́ изви́листо не́сколькими рукава́ми.

[9] *R.S.* 26 (ii).

[10] куда́ река́ уходи́ла.

[11] ра́зве лишь с одного́ ме́ста avoids the ambiguity of за исключе́нием одного́ ме́ста. Notice this combination of ра́зве лишь (ра́зве то́лько) in the meaning of е́сли не 'if not', 'unless'.

[12] свиде́тельствовали о . . .

[13] то . . . и зате́м . . .

[14] по́сле холодо́в. *R.S.* 19 (iii).

[15] сквозь проры́вы в клубя́щихся облака́х.

[16] They actually were thrust: hence вонза́лись, or a similar verb. One might say с пронза́вшими его наскво́зь.

# 98

We live on a large farm in southern Tuscany—twelve miles from[1] the station and five from the nearest village. The country[2] is wild and lonely: the climate harsh. Our house stands on a hillside, looking down over[3] a wide and beautiful valley, beyond which rises Monte Amiata, wooded with[4] chestnuts and beeches. Nearer by, on this side[5] of the valley, lie slopes of cultivated land[6]—wheat, olives, and vines. Among them still stand some ridges of dust-coloured[7] clay[8] hillocks, the *crete senesi*, as bare and colourless as elephants' backs, as mountains of the moon. The wide river-bed in the valley holds[9] a rushing stream in the rainy season, but during the summer a mere trickle, in a wide desert of stones.[10] Then, when the wheat ripens and the alfalfa has been cut, the last patches of green disappear from the landscape. The whole valley becomes dust-coloured[11]—a land without mercy, without shade.[12] If you sit under an olive tree you are not shaded; the leaves are like little flickering tongues of fire. At evening and morning the distant hills are misty and blue, but under one's feet the dry earth is hard. The cry of cicadas shrills[13] in the noonday. One can only wait—anxiously, thirstily[14]—for the September rains, when the whole countryside comes to life again. The vintage comes, the ox-carts[15] are piled high with purple and yellow grapes. The farmhouses and the trees around them are hung with[16] the last vestiges of the harvest.

IRIS ORIGO

1 Usə в + prep. to express the distance of one object from another.

2 'Country', 'terrain', and 'locality' are all suggested by мéстность.

3 и смóтрит вниз на . . .

4 Make adjectives from the trees and say 'covered with chestnut and beech woods' (покры́тый + instr.).

5 Idiomatically по э́ту стóрону. *R.S.* 569.

6 This can be translated literally, with the crops in the genitive case in apposition: склóны воздéланной земли́ — пшени́цы . . .

7 пы́льного цвéта or цвéта пы́ли.

8 гли́нистый, i.e. 'containing clay', 'clayey', not гли́няный 'fabricated from clay'.

9 Not дéржит. One might say ширóкое ру́сло реки́ вмещáет . . . потóк . . .; но лéтом он превращáется в стру́йку . . . Or perhaps по ширóкому ру́слу реки́ стреми́тся (бурли́т) потóк; но лéтом . . .

10 Say 'stony desert' среди́ . . . камени́стой пусты́ни. Cf. камени́стый 'consisting wholly or partly of stones' and кáменный 'fabricated from stone', 'stone-like', 'to do with stone'; and see *R.S.* 160 for other examples.

11 Станóвится пы́льного цвéта, or alternatively приобретáет пы́льную окрáску.

12 Say 'it does not give shade'.

13 Say 'cicadas cry shrilly'. Use the verb стрекотáть.

14 There is no single adverb for 'thirstily'. Use с + instr. (e.g. с вожделéнием which is better here than с жáждой) and precede it by с нетерпéнием to keep the parallelism of the two English adverbs.

15 Say 'the yoked-by-oxen carts' запряжённые волáми телéги.

16 'To hang' (transitive) is вéшать (повéсить); cf. 'to hang' (intransitive) висéть. 'To hang something with', 'hang something on', 'cover something with hanging objects' is увéшивать (увéшать). Here use the short form of the past participle passive, followed by the instrumental case.

## 99

One of the hardest things[1] to remember is that a man's merit[2] in one sphere is no guarantee of his merit in another. Newton's mathematics don't prove his theology. Faraday was right about[3] electricity, but not about Sandemanism. Plato wrote marvellously well and that's why people still go on believing in his pernicious philosophy. Tolstoy was an excellent novelist; but that's no reason for[4] regarding his ideas about morality as anything but[5] detestable, or for feeling anything but contempt for his aesthetics, his sociology, and his religion.[6] In the case of[7] scientists and philosophers, this ineptitude outside their own line of business isn't surprising. Indeed, it's almost inevitable. For it's obvious that excessive development of the purely mental functions leads to atrophy of all the rest. Hence the notorious infantility of professors and ludicrous simplicity of the solutions they offer for the problems of life. But in an artist there's less specialization, less one-sided development; consequently, the artist oughtn't to have the blind spots and the imbecilities[8] of the philosophers and saints. That's why a man like Tolstoy is so specially unforgivable. Instinctively you trust him more than you would trust an intellectual. And there he goes perverting[9] all his deepest instincts and being just as idiotic and pernicious as St. Francis of Assisi, or as Kant the moralist (oh, those categorical imperatives! and then the fact that the only thing the old gentleman felt at all deeply about was crystallized fruit!),[10] or Newton the theologian.

ALDOUS HUXLEY

[1] Say simply труднée всегó.

[2] Either спосóбности 'abilities' or достижéния 'achievements' would be appropriate here.

[3] прав относи́тельно.

[4] э́то не даёт основáний + infinitive.

[5] считáть . . . чéм-либо ины́м, как.

[6] Make adjectives from the nouns and combine them with взгля́ды.

[7] по отношéнию к + dat.

[8] In the absence of a literal equivalent for 'blind spots', one might say пробе́лы в зна́ниях. 'Imbecilities' — вздо́рные выска́зывания . . .

[9] а он возьми́ да (и) изврати́. See *R.S.* 282 for this modal use of the imperative, and continue: и ведёт себя́ так же по-идио́тски, &c.

[10] Be careful of the agreement when translating by some such phrase as еди́нственное, что глубоко́ волнова́ло . . . бы́ли заса́харенные фру́кты.

# 100

Reading for pleasure and reading for profit is a distinction which most people, presumably, can maintain[1] all their lives, and if it is lost it is because reading becomes wholly a spare-time[2] occupation. But the professional man of letters finds himself in a more pitiful condition; all he reads must be grist to his mill[3] and it is rarely that he can afford himself the time to read for no purpose at all beyond[4] immediate enjoyment.[5] Sometimes, however, time and circumstances leave him stranded.[6] He picks up what is at hand, and reads idly, innocently, incontinently.[7] In such a mood I recently found myself indulging[8]—I was conscious of the moral aspect—in a recently published novel. There is no point in divulging[9] its name, but it was a clever novel, by one of the most promising of our younger writers. I was absorbed, and finished the book before the long summer's day was over. I was very pleased, and promised myself to read more modern fiction. The experience had been vivid, and for the moment the characters in the book haunted me with their glittering presences.[10] For the moment! For the day being a long one, I turned[11] in the evening to another book, a book I had read years ago and which I had often intended to re-read—Stendhal's Journal, which he called *Vie de Henri Brulard*. I had not read many of its not very exciting pages before[12] I realized that the experience was totally different in kind from the experience of the earlier part of the day; and that before the reality of this experience, the art of the novelist had collapsed like a pack of slippery cards.

HERBERT READ

[1] i.e. 'keep to', 'hold to': придéрживаться + gen.

[2] In the absence of a single word equivalent, some circumlocution is necessary; e.g. котóрому отвóдят часы́ досýга.

[3] Some possible translations are: всё должнó лить вóду на егó мéльницу; он дóлжен всё перемолóть на своéй мéльнице; or, departing from the image, из всегó, что он читáет, он дóлжен извлéчь вы́году.

[4] еди́нственно с цéлью.

[5] Say 'to enjoy it at the present moment'.

[6] Here the meaning is not 'let him down' (подвóдят егó), but rather 'leave him with some time on his hands'; e.g. оставля́ют емý свобóдную минýту.

[7] If the alliteration is to be kept, one might say: беспéчно, без зáдних мы́слей, безýдержно.

[8] Say 'finding myself in such a mood I indulged' (увлёкся).

[9] приводи́ть (привести́) 'to adduce' or 'cite' would be a good alternative to a verb 'to disclose'.

[10] неотвя́зно стоя́ли пéредо мной в своём блистáтельном обли́чьи. Обли́чье is a somewhat rhetorical alternative of óблик, and would be in place here.

[11] Say 'the day dragged out a long time, and I turned' (взялся́ за).

[12] не успéл я . . . как . . .

PRINTED IN GREAT BRITAIN
AT THE UNIVERSITY PRESS, OXFORD
BY VIVIAN RIDLER
PRINTER TO THE UNIVERSITY